WHEN FRIDAY NIGHT WAS COUNTY NIGHT

Stockport Footballing Memories

Barry Cheetham

Published by Sigma Leisure – an imprint of
Sigma Press, 1 South Oak Lane, Wilmslow, Cheshire SK9 6AR, England.

British Library Cataloguing in Publication Data
A CIP record for this book is available from the British Library.

ISBN: 1-85058-719-1

Typesetting and Design by: Sigma Press, Wilmslow, Cheshire.

Printed by: MFP Design & Print

Cover Design: Design House

Preface

The book is a personalised history of Stockport County FC which spans a period of 46 years (1952-1998), although the events described do not appear in chronological order.

It deals with some of the things that happened to the club and its supporters during the last fairly successful decade but the emphasis is upon the era when watching County was a duty rather than a pleasure, during the '60s, '70s and '80s – *When Friday Night was County Night.*

I hope that supporters of other clubs, as well as County fans of course, will feel that they are able to identify with the characters and feelings described.

It is also a little bit about friendship. The seven people quoted on the fronting page started to go to Edgeley Park as a group when they were teenagers in the early 1960s. Now, as middle aged men, we still remain in contact and are still good friends. Even though some of us have lived away from Stockport between then and now, County has always been a shared interest and a common denominator in our lives and is a major reason why we are still in touch.

Sadly, we now number only six. In October 1998, David Booth died after a brave battle against cancer. This is the reason why I felt moved to write this book. I would like to dedicate it to David in recognition of his courage and humanity.

I have pledged much of any royalties which may come my way to cancer charities.

Barry Cheetham

Acknowledgements

Special thanks to Richard Harnwell for the photographs.
Thanks also to Paul Angus for help with the computer!

100 Years of Quotations

"What have you done, you over there,
crying bitter tears,
Tell me, what have you done, you over there,
With your youthful years?"
Paul Verlaine. (1899)

"Spent a lot of them supporting a lost cause." – *Barry Cheetham (1980)*

"Referee, blow for half-time. The fans need a rest." – *Stuart Hart (1974)*

" When my kids misbehave, I just threaten to take them to County."
– *Gerry McEvoy (1978)*

"We promise we'll be good, dad." – *Paul and Simon McEvoy (1978)*

"I bet he even missed the last episode of 'The Fugitive'." (As a penalty landed on the railway lines.) – *Mick Orr (1961)*

"It's a good job County won." (Gurgled through a mass of stitches in his face and mouth after a road accident). – *John Henshaw (1967)*

"George Best playing for County? It's like Toscanini making a record with Slade." – *Lawson Shield (1975)*

"Get up Sandiford. You're not hurt! (As Trevor Porteous lay doubled over in agony so that his number 6 was displayed upside down.) – *David Thompson (1964)*

"Just warming my hands on your ear." (After a desperate clearance from Andy Thorpe had smacked into the side of my face on a freezing February afternoon). – *David Booth (1990)*

"Do you think we should sign Verlaine, Harry?" – *Former County manager (1998)*

Contents

1. *So Long, Batman* 1

2. *George Best – The Glory Hours* 7

3. *Danny Who?* 11
– includes transcript of interview with Danny Bergara, recorded 18th July 1989

4. *Halifax Town 1, Alan Ogley 0* 16

5. *In the Shadow of Stretford* 20

6. *Flight of The Albatross (1964-65)* 23

7. *When Friday Night Was County Night – Part 1* 30

8. *When Friday Night Was County Night – Part 2* 36

9. *Wembley Blues* 42

10. *Favourite Goals* 45

11. *Charlie's Penalty and a Dirty Trick* 50

12. *Raw Deals* 53

13. *Fifty Miles Wide* 56

14. *When Friday Night Was County Night – Part 3* 71

15. *Heroes in Adversity* 74

16. *The Great Escape* 85

17. *The Friendly Football Club* 92

18. *"We Had Joy, We Had Fun, We Had Seasons In The Sun ..."* 97

19. *The Dirtiest Foul of Them All* 125

20. *A Tangled Wilderness and a 60-Year Dream* 126

21. *A Worthy Knight and a Portaloo* 133

22. *Where Do We Go From Here?* 136

1

So Long, Batman

Every Saturday between August and May, some kid will go along to a football match for the first time. The chances are that thereafter this child will become addicted to following the fortunes of the chosen team through ups and downs, season after season with the same childlike anticipation once adulthood has been reached. It won't matter where that person may live in the future or whether or not they can attend many matches. The affiliation will remain with the person always.

My first ever visit to Edgeley Park happened purely by chance. It was a murky Saturday in early November 1952 – one of those days when autumn is about to give way to winter, with just a slight breeze to disturb the fallen leaves, yet chilly enough to carry with it the warning of approaching winter and the smoke of bonfire night – and in those days smoke also from the factory chimneys that dominated the skyline of many towns in the north of England.

Four seven year old boys were on their way to Mersey Square, enough money in their pockets to pay for admission to the Plaza matinee, a few sweets and a couple of ice lollies. As the bus pulled up at the end of Merseyway, Alan had what he thought was a brilliant idea. Showing that night at the Plaza was a western that we all wanted to see. Unfortunately for us the film was 'A' rated, which meant that we could only get in if accompanied by an adult. The bright idea was to watch the usual "Tanner Rush" offerings of "Hopalong Cassidy", "Batman" and "Woody Woodpecker", and then hide in the loo until the first house started before sneaking back into the auditorium to watch the film. Mike and myself were not convinced about the viability of this stratagem.

The outcome was a heated argument conducted alongside the high railings above the exquisitely perfumed Mersey. Alan and the other Alan decided that Mike and myself were totally chicken and stormed off to join the queue for what was probably Episode 45 of "Batman" etc.

"Didn't really fancy the pictures anyway," I said, "Shall we do somethin' else?"

While Mike and I were considering how best we might spend Saturday afternoon, we noticed that quite a lot of people were boarding a bus bearing the sign "FOOTBALL SPECIAL" at the other side of the Square near the Bear Pit. On a mad impulse we joined the exodus to Edgeley.

Having arrived at the top end of Castle Street, we followed the crowd and finished up in the Cheadle End, an interesting enclosure in those days with its wooden terracing with an inch wide slit in the middle.

Because we were small, we were allowed to move near to the front and managed to squeeze in right behind the goal. A lot of the other kids were wearing black and white scarves and brandishing rattles which they swung round from time to time, creating quite an interesting noise. We were aware that County were about to play Workington, having clubbed together to buy a programme. We were amused to learn that County would be wearing "white shirts and black knickers" and that Workington would be in "red shirts and white knickers". (And Ruud Gullit thought he had invented sexy football).

It had started to become misty and gloomy by the time the players took the field, although it was still early afternoon, games starting at 2.15 at that time of year, in the pre-floodlight era.

And so the match began ... County were kicking towards the Railway End and were having most of the play. Straining our eyes to see through the netting, we could make out small figures in white and red shirts and a figure clad in green and white who seemed to be diving about all over the place.

This was, in contrast to the green-jerseyed figure in front of us, one Jack "Tiger" Bowles, who seemed to have a great relationship with the people behind his goal. He chatted amiably with the fans on the occasions when he wasn't prowling around the penalty area in the fashion that had earned him his nickname – yet never crossing over the boundaries of the area as though the line markings were the boundaries of his tiger's cage.

The approving cheers and roars of the crowd were evidence even to such inexperienced spectators as Mike and myself that things were going well for the home team. As half-time approached County led

"Sorry lads – I forgot to bring the dice" – in training, 1953

2-0 and it appeared that someone named Jack Connor had scored both goals. Even so, we were beginning to get a bit bored, unable as we were to work out exactly what was happening at the other end of the field. Edgeley Park, notorious for being one of the smallest surfaces on which professional football is played, seemed to be an immense terrain to a seven-year-old peering through the gloom, the netting and the legs of Jack Bowles.

Suddenly the Workington goalkeeper dived full length, collided with one of the white-shirted figures and stayed on the ground. The match stopped for a few minutes while a track-suited figure wearing a flat cap raced onto the field carrying a bucket. After he had administered some form of first aid to the stricken goalkeeper, the game recommenced for a few more minutes before a long blast from the referee's whistle signalled half-time.

During the interval, I was wondering whether we would have been better off at the Plaza. Most of the action had been at the other end of the field. Jack Bowles was interesting enough and had even dealt competently with a couple of shots and centres before belting the ball once more into the distance and the mist. However, what I had seen

The first of five for Jack Connor ...

so far did not compare very favourably with the action on the large screen at the Plaza cinema.

But what a change was to come! Out came the players for the second half. The Workington goalkeeper had his left hand heavily bandaged. Apparently, he had dived at the feet of a County forward and for his pains (literally) had received a few leather studs in the back of his hand.

The game became quite exciting as County mounted attack after attack. Another goal soon arrived. What a wonderful sight it was to see the roof of the net bulge as the number 10 (Andy Black) blasted home a shot from about 10 yards. A few minutes later the valiant Workington keeper (I think his name was Newlands) needed further attention, having flung himself to his left to turn aside a fierce shot and deny Jack Connor his hat-trick. Blood started to seep through the bandage at the back and stain the sleeve of his Jersey. (Real blood. Wow! This is better than Hopalong Cassidy!)

This courageous act was in vain, however, as Jack Connor duly completed his hat-trick, a deft flick of his Brylcreemed head dispatching the ball firmly into the bottom corner of the net. He accepted with

... and the fifth!

suave equanimity the handshakes and backslaps of his team-mates. In those days, there was no kissing of colleagues or shirts. The brave Newlands made several more fine saves and earned the admiration of both County fans and players but was unable to prevent Jack Connor from scoring twice more.

I can't remember the last two goals but what does stick in my mind is the fact that my new-found hero went straight up to the goalkeeper at the end of the match to congratulate him on his courageous performance. The track-suited figure with the flat cap also came up to the goalkeeper and the three men walked off the field together.

When I witness some of the things that go on in football some forty odd years later, I think that it's a great pity that young people of today are denied the type of role model that Jack Connor provided for me on that fateful day.

We wriggled through the thronging mass at the gates and ran down to Mersey Square, passing underneath the station – one part of Stockport which has not changed much in all those years. By the time we reached Mersey Square, the "tanner rush" had long since finished and the queues were forming outside the Plaza for the first house of the western. Wondering whether the two Alans were soon to emerge from their noxious hiding place into the darkness of the auditorium, we boarded the number 17 bus to return to our South Reddish homes. We little realised that, shortly afterwards, the great man himself would be catching the same bus, living as he did a little further up the road towards Houldsworth Square. As the bus pulled out to turn right into Prince's Street, I glanced back in the direction of the Plaza – no more Saturday matinees for me – the new crusader didn't wear a cape, but a white shirt with a black number nine on the back.

2

George Best – The Glory Hours

It may seem strange nowadays to think of a local hero using public transport. However, there was one County player who certainly didn't have to catch the bus and who was more of a national institution than a local hero.

I can't remember the actual circumstances which led to George Best playing three times at Edgeley Park in late 1975 – only that he was not employed by any other club and that someone at County (Dragan Lukic?) had had an absolute brainwave. In any event, one Friday night in late November, a crowd of over 9,000, almost treble the normal gate, packed into the crumbling infrastructure of Edgeley Park to see the maestro make his debut for the home team against Swansea City. Looking decidedly unfit and even disinterested, George had played no major part in the proceedings until County were awarded a corner at the Railway End. George swung a right-footed inswinger towards the near post. The Swansea defenders scrambled the ball away for another corner which resulted in a repeat performance. George tried again. This time he swerved the ball straight into the net at the far post. What a genius! The crowd went mad. County went on to scramble a 3-2 victory. If my memory serves me well, the winning goal was scored by Lee Bradley, a youngster who, like his contemporary, Steve Massey, failed to fulfil his early promise – hardly surprising when you are learning about professional football in such a disadvantageous environment as Edgeley Park was in those days.

The fact that George Best was contracted to play in home games only may have had a detrimental effect on team spirit because the following week County were trounced 5-0 at Reading. This unfortunate result kept the crowd down to more manageable proportions for the visit of Watford the following Friday when George obliged with another goal in a 2-2 draw.

George made what proved to be his final appearance for County on Boxing Day and played his part in a somewhat fortunate 1-0 win over

Ouch!

Southport in a match which, for some inexplicable reason, kicked off at 11 o' clock. The "Scourge of Benfica" appeared looking decidedly pale, as though he had just got out of bed and was suffering from the mother of all hangovers. (The same could perhaps be said of most of the crowd). He was unable to make much of a contribution to the cause, because every time he received the ball, he found himself closely marked by the Southport players.

Suddenly, however, he sprang to life. It was as though a message had been transmitted into his brain – you can beat this lot on your bloody own! – and, for a few precious moments, the genius was born again. Having for once received a half-decent pass, he proceeded to dribble nonchalantly past four opponents before rolling the ball across the six yard box for a County forward to come running up and belt the ball into the car park behind the Cheadle End. George hung his head in despair. His chin was nearly touching his beer gut. Standing next to me was a long-term friend and fellow County fan called Gerard McEvoy. Gerry turned to me and with an expression of wounded resignation on his face, said quietly, "He used to make chances like that for Denis Law."

"You can't take three successive corners and try to score with each one."

"Who can't?"

The match sank back to its previous level of mediocrity and George Best went through the motions of playing out the remainder of the 90 minutes, probably dreaming of a warm bed with a Miss World in it. The maestro had helped us to a 1-0 win but he had played his last game for County.

The club wanted George to play on New Year's Day against a strong Cambridge United side who were pushing for promotion under the guidance of their former player, Ron Atkinson. I fail to recall whether George refused to play or whether he just failed to turn up. All I remember about the match is a 1-0 defeat on a gluepot of a pitch and a disgraceful racist gesture by a certain County player which resulted in the unfortunate dismissal of Brendan Batson for retaliation.

In a recent football programme, a round-up of the weekend's matches involving local clubs, George Best was the special guest whose job it was to comment on the matches and to make passing reference to some of the highlights of his career at Manchester United and Fulham. No mention was made of his brief spell as a County player. Just as when he walked off Edgeley Park for the last time, George appeared to be a bit uncomfortable, probably embarrassed by the "tour de force" of unctious grovelling on the part of the programme's presenter, whose sycophantic attempts to ingratiate himself with his guest made Uriah Heap look like Wat Tyler.

Anyway, thanks for the memory, George. For just a short while, in those desperate times of the mid 1970s, Edgeley Park was an exciting place. Brendan Batson and servile interviewing form the tenuous link with the next chapter.

3

Danny Who?

In March 1989, Brendan Ellwood and his fellow directors took the decision to dispense with the services of Asa Hartford and appoint one Alberto Daniel Bergara, at the time managing Rochdale, in his place.

This managerial change was not well-received by the majority of fans. Hartford, in his prime an excellent player, had been quite popular and it was felt that he had done a reasonable job in keeping the club away from non-league football on the limited budget at his disposal. Furthermore, County had recently defeated a very poor Rochdale side by 3-0, the most comfortable of the ten league victories achieved that season.

Bergara's reign at Edgeley Park did not begin very auspiciously. In charge for the last eleven games of the season, the man from Montevideo watched his side draw seven times and lose four. This did not compare at all favourably with his predecessor's record of: Won 10, Drawn 14, Lost 11. During this unsuccessful conclusion to the season, the new manager constantly changed the combination of strikers in order, he claimed, that he might be able to see who the best ones were. Without doubt, in my opinion, the best one by far was the soon to retire and become physio Rodger Wylde, who had been out of favour/injured up to the demise of the previous regime. Wylde was recalled briefly only to be replaced by a clumsy-looking individual called Brett Angell, who had been signed by Asa Hartford for the then club record fee of £32,000. The other available forwards (Colville, Caldwell and Hancock) all seemed to be better prospects than Angell who, since making his debut the previous autumn, had been in and out of the team and had managed to score just four goals. Early the following season, he was to double his tally in just one match! I can remember being similarly unimpressed with Mick Quinn and Kevin Francis when I first saw them play!

It was through professional reasons that I contacted Edgeley Park in the summer of 1989. (I was involved in an educational project and needed some information about Uruguay). I telephoned the club and was asked to write to the manager requesting an interview. This I duly did and my eleven year old son, himself a true devotee of the cause, arrived home from school one afternoon just in time to answer the telephone. He was quite amazed to find himself in conversation with the County manager! Fortunately, he was able to keep his wits about him and note down the direct line to ring in order to speak with Danny Bergara. I rang the number and was able to fix up the interview which follows. I wanted some information about what life was like in Uruguay in the 1950s. All I could get him to talk about was football! Before switching on the tape, I asked Danny Bergara about a photograph on his desk. This prompted him to give a warm tribute to the late Harry Haslam, who had been his mentor, employing him at Luton Town and Sheffield United. Apparently, when Danny had first come to England, life had not been easy.

Transcript of interview with Danny Bergara, recorded 18th July 1989

BC: Could you give me some brief details about yourself?

DB: I was born in Montevideo, republic of Uruguay in 1942. When I was 14, I was signed up by Racing Club of Montevideo. I made my debut in the Uruguayan first division at the age of 16. When I was 17, I played for the international youth team against Argentina twice and against Chile. When I was 20, the coach of Real Mallorca, Jose Luis Saso, negotiated with Racing Club for my transfer and I decided to go to play football in Mallorca.

BC: Could you tell me a little bit about your childhood?

DB: Yes. When I was very small, my father bought a farm at Tapia, an area about 25 kilometres outside Montevideo. My father was a "gaucho" – the city life was not for him. Actually, he didn't own the farm by himself – it was in partnership with his brother. My father wanted to own his own ranch, and so we moved to Rocha on the Atlantic coast. There, we lived on the "estancia". My father rented the land but owned all the livestock. We also grew wheat, barley, sunflowers, watermelons and vegetables. Unfortunately, in 1949 my father died. My mother kept the place going until 1953. In fact, she didn't sell it until 1955, but a foreman ran the place for the last two years. Possibly because Mum thought it would be better for our education, we moved back to Montevideo in 1953. We all lived in Montevideo and Mum used to go back to the ranch every one or two months to see how things were going. I was enrolled in the "Colegio Pio" with the Salesian fathers. It was there that I was encouraged to play football. The Salesian order is famous for encouraging young people to do sport.

BC: Did you enjoy life at the "Colegio Pio"?

DB: It was good. I enjoyed it very much. The only problem was that every single day you had to go to Mass in the morning and in the evening. For six years I went to Mass twice a day. I think I've put enough Masses in the bank to last me, so now I rarely go.

BC: In other words your religion now is football?

DB: Yes. That's right. My church is the office of the club where I work. (Note: Danny Bergara was to become renowned for comments of an architectural nature in his programme notes.)

BC: What did it feel like when you left Uruguay for the first time?

DB: As I said, Jose Luis Saso persuaded me to go to Mallorca and play in the Spanish first division. So I arrived in Mallorca on 8 August 1962, still wearing my winter clothes.

BC: It must have been quite an experience for a young man of 20.

DB: Unforgettable. I'd never been away from my family before. Mum had been very protective since Dad's death. When you're 20 and have the world at your feet, you tend not to think. Then, suddenly, you find yourself at the other side of the world on your own and you realise how much you miss your family. So Mallorca was a very big step for me and I'll always remember it. But, as a young man, you can only dream of playing in the Bernabeu Stadium or Nou Camp – now, for me that was about to become reality. And it was in Mallorca where I met my wife. She worked for a travel company as a secretary and a guide for six months during the summer season. She used to work in Mallorca for six months and then go back to London in the winter.

BC: Your wife is English, then? (Thick question)

DB: Yes. Born in Hampstead.

BC: How long did you stay in Mallorca?

DB: Five years. The first two years were very difficult because I was used to a type of football which was slower and more technical and perhaps not as well-organised as the Spanish game. It took me two years to get into the rhythm of it properly.

(At this point the telephone rang and Danny Bergara spoke to Brendan Batson of the PFA. It was to do with someone being in breach of contract. – Enough said.)

DB: I made my debut against Athletic Bilbao and we won 1-0 and I'll never forget the second game I played. It was against Real Madrid on 31 December 1962. We won 5-2 and I scored the fifth goal. Their side included Santamaria, Pachin, Zoco, Munoz, Puskas and Gento. Di Stefano didn't play. He was injured. I played ten games in my first season. In those days, they only played 30 league games each season. In my second season, I only played a dozen or so games and we were relegated to the second division. At that time, my brother Ignacio, "Nacho", came to Spain to play for Espanol. He is now the coach at Algeciras. In my third season, we had Cesar Rodriguez in charge. He's a great coach and a wonderful person. We won the championship of the second division south and then beat Pontevedra, the northern section champions, to become overall champions. During that season and the next two, I was leading goalscorer for the club.

BC: Which club did you play for after leaving Real Mallorca?

DB: I was transferred to Sevilla for 2,500,000 pesetas plus one of their players – so the whole fee would be 3,500,000 (about £25,000), which was quite a big fee in those days. In fact, it was, at the time, the record transfer fee that Real Mallorca had received.

BC: Did you have much success in Sevilla?

DB: A fair bit. I wouldn't say a lot. In my first season, we were relegated. The following season we came up as champions and I was leading scorer again. That season we had Max Merked, a German, who had been coach at Munich 1860 when they lost in the Cup Winners' Cup Final to West Ham. With Max in charge we finished third in the first division and seventh the following season. The year after, I left Sevilla.

BC: Where did you go next?

DB: To Tenerife. We had a couple of reasonable seasons but then ended up in the relegation play-offs. It was in one of those matches that I received the injury that ended my career. (He pulled up his trouser leg to reveal a scar stretching from knee to ankle).

BC: What did you do in the years between finishing as a footballer and becoming a coach?

DB: Since my wife is English, we decided to come to England and I worked for a while in the travel business. Unfortunately, those were the days of power cuts and three day working weeks and I wasn't a success to say the least. It was then that I met Harry Haslam and he gave me my big chance, working at Luton Town. I followed Harry to Sheffield United, had a spell at Middlesborough, and then came back to Sheffield United for another two years. I also became coach of the England Youth team – the only Latin American in the history of football to be involved with an English national team – I'm very proud of that achievement. Then I was offered the job of managing Rochdale. Things went quite well there at first but they didn't treat me very well as regards contracts. So, when Stockport offered me the post of manager, I decided to come here, where I hope to achieve some success.

BC: The fans of Stockport County hope you do as well.

DB: Thank you. My other ambition is to become the first South American to lead an English team on to the pitch at Wembley......

BC: (Thinks) Now that is going a bit beyond the bounds of reality.

Paul Jones, the player coach, came into the office at that moment and we spent another hour or so talking about football and some more of Danny's experiences playing in Spain. (I had actually seen him play for Sevilla against Atletico Madrid).

His enthusiasm was so infectious that I left Edgeley Park with the feeling that maybe, just maybe, here was the man who was about to change the fortunes of Stockport County. The hospitality that the manager had shown me prompted me to write a letter in support of him to the "Stockport Express". The letter was published in the week before the first match of the new season. I was given a great deal of "stick" by the cynics with whom I used to stand on the terraces. Little did they, or I, know at the start of the 1989-90 season that the next five years were to be such a roller coaster ride of extremes of triumph and despair. Without doubt, 1996-97 was to be the best ever season in terms of achievement and, at the time of writing, County are more than holding their own in the first division. However, it is Danny Bergara who will always be remembered by the County faithful as the man who brought hope back to Edgeley Park.

After some time spent watching teams such as Real and Atletico Madrid, during the time when Danny played for Real Mallorca and Sevilla, I returned to this country in time for what, in my opinion, was County's worst season ever.

4

Halifax Town 1, Alan Ogley 0

It had been a great summer. Young, single and in gainful employment, John Henshaw and myself had just returned from a trip to the south of France, where we had been guests at a wedding, Andorra, Spain and Portugal.

This meant that we had missed the start of the 1969-70 season. Because of the World Cup, which would take place in Mexico in June 1970, the first matches were played on 9 August 1969. On that day, in the company of the aforementioned Henshaw, I was the "temoin" at the wedding of my great friends Geoff and Maite Shooter in the small Arieges village of Mercenac. As Henshaw and I enjoyed the wedding celebrations in the glorious sunshine of southern France, we were blissfully unaware of the fact that in the somewhat less idyllic surroundings of Birkenhead, County were receiving a 3-0 drubbing at the hands of Tranmere Rovers.

In those days, communication was a lot more difficult than it is now and it was not until the following week, in Oporto of all places, that we learned of County's dreadful start to the season.

However, a few days later, after we had spent some time in Lisbon, an event occurred which cheered us up immensely. Accompanying us on this stage of the trip was another old pal of mine, Roger Brett, aka Brett Rogers on the occasions when he would attempt to supplement his student grant by reinventing himself as a fourth rate pub singer. In spite of the fact that Roger Brett Rogers is a southerner and a Brentford fan, Henshaw and I had agreed to let him travel with us. We were glad that he did so because it was he who suggested a trip to see the home of Benfica, the famous Stadium of Light.

We parked up in front of the stadium and walked below the famous Eagles into the domain of Portugal's most famous club. Amazingly, no-one was there to either welcome us or throw us out and it wasn't long before we found ourselves wandering out on to the pitch itself. We were hailed by three young groundsmen who were preparing the pitch for the coming season. In my faltering Portuguese, I managed to communicate to them that we had come to pay homage to Eusebio, Torres, Simoes, etc., and they seemed to be quite pleased that we had bothered to look the place up.

The groundsmen had a football and soon a scratch game developed in the ungroomed half of the pitch with the actual, real Benfica goal at one end and bags put down to mark the goal defended by Stockport County/ Brentford. At first, the Benfica groundsmen played us off the park, as we struggled to put our game together in the midday heat of Lisbon. We were losing 6-0 but, soon afterwards, we transformed the scoreline to 10-6 in our favour, with a hat-trick each from Henshaw and myself and four from Brett. Whether this was due to magnificent British fighting spirit or the fact that the groundsmen were trying to eat their lunch, I would rather not say. The match came to an abrupt end when I awarded myself a fairly dubious penalty. I decided to be crafty and take it quickly while the Benfica goalkeeper was sinking his teeth into a gargantuan sandwich. In my haste, I blasted the ball too near the keeper who stuck out a hand to palm the ball away, with the result that the vast majority of his massive butty was sent splattering into the back of the goal. One of their side raced upfield and reduced the arrears to 10-7. It was at this point that we were told that we would have to go as the foreman would soon be back from his lunch.

We duly complied with the request of our affable hosts, bade them a cheery farewell and boarded the team's Mark 1 Cortina to head vaguely in the direction of Coimbra.

In spite of the heroic exploits of my two team mates, I think that I can boast, without fear of contradiction, that I am the only Englishman to score a hat-trick *and* miss a penalty in Lisbon's Stadium of Light.

Homeward bound towards the end of August, we learned that the first victory (and goal as well) had been achieved – a 1-0 win over Gillingham.

Elated by this cheering news, we arrived back in Stockport too late to witness the 1-0 defeat at the hands of Torquay. This meant that the first chance we would have of watching the team play would be at Halifax on 6 September. Henshaw and myself, keen to see a game, were able only with difficulty to persuade the rest of our usual companions to make the short trip to West Yorkshire. The others had watched the defeats at Tranmere and Barnsley as well as the fairly miserable home performances.

The writing had been on the wall for some time. Jimmy Meadows had left and the managerial reigns were in the hands of Walter Galbraith, whose track record did not exactly inspire confidence. Jim Fryatt and Bill Atkins had been sold. Len Allchurch and Alex Young (the "Golden Vision" to Everton fans – the "Golden Wheelchair" to County fans) had both retired. The club was left with only a handful of decent players: Alan Ogley in goal, the consistent Billy Haydock and his full-back partner, Barry Hartle, Freddie Goodwin in midfield, forward John Rowlands and winger John Price, the smallest player in league football, were all good players. The rest weren't.

Later in the season, former England international, Peter Broadbent was signed from Wolves, a young player called Jimmy Collier, who looked to be quite promising was drafted in to the first team and Hughie Ryden rejoined the club from Halifax Town. Even with these reinforcements, County were unable to stop the rot.

I think that Hughie played against us in that match at the Shay and, like the other Halifax players that afternoon, left the pitch wondering how they had only managed to win 1-0. Only four of County's outfield players (Price, Haydock, Hartle and Goodwin) seemed interested. The others might as well have come and stood next to us. Halifax were enjoying possibly their best ever season under the guidance of Alan Ball senior and their failure to exact full retribution for that famous 13-0 defeat in 1934 was due mainly to the heroics of goalkeeper Ogley.

Alan Ogley may not have been the best goalkeeper County have ever had but there have certainly been none braver. I have seen him pick up some nasty injuries and remember one match in particular when play was held up for several minutes while officials and players searched the goalmouth mud for his contact lenses!

Fortunately for County, Ogley was able to play in every single match that season. Luck in that respect was on his side at least, risking as he did life and limb attempting to keep the score down to reasonable proportions in the majority of games. The game at the Shay was probably his best ever performance for County with the league cup-tie against West Ham three years later coming a close second.

Including the league cup game against Blackburn (0-2), that was County's seventh match of the season and they had scored just one goal. Shell-shocked, we drove back to Stockport. Twenty years later, we would drive back from Halifax in a similar state of mind but for very different reasons.

In the autumn of 1969, as Enoch Powell made his infamous "Rivers of Blood" speech and consigned himself to political oblivion, County failed to score in eight of their first ten matches and consigned themselves to footballing oblivion. They managed a total of 27 in the league, just over half a goal per game. Although this was the Third Division, it was still more excruciating to watch than even our worst performances in the fourth.

Perhaps the FA Cup would bring some much needed relief and revenue, as it had done five years earlier. Dream on! In the First Round, County managed to account for non-league Mossley by 1-0 in a replay, having been fortunate to scrape a 1-1 draw in the first match at Edgeley Park. In the second round, Fourth Division Scunthorpe were the visitors, riding high in the league and favourites to go through, even though by then County had actually managed to win 1-0 in two consecutive matches.

The sides fought out a 0-0 draw at Edgeley Park and I can remember being impressed by three of their players – a tricky winger called Harry Kirk, an accomplished looking defender called Steven Deere and a busy little forward wearing the number eight shirt. Ironically, both Kirk and Deere were later to play for County. Kevin Keegan, on the other hand, preferred to go and play for Liverpool; but not before scoring twice in the 4-0 mauling that Scunthorpe administered in the replay.

After Freddie Goodwin was sold to Blackburn at the end of February, County managed one win and two draws from their last fourteen matches – a truly putrid end to the most putrid of seasons. Practically relegated by the end of August, they had managed to amass (for want of a better word) a grand total of 23 points. Half a point and half a goal per match, a P45 for Walter and a return to Division Four to spend the next 20 years as the country's most unsuccessful league club. I summoned up the courage to go and watch the last game of the season. It was the return fixture of match number one and that meant another two points for Tranmere. It was late April, 1970. The next Third Division match at Edgeley Park would take place on 17 August 1991. As Tranmere strolled to their inevitable 1-0 victory, a group of drunken County fans in front of us chanted a mournful dirge:

"What keeps us keeping on?
To see Stockport County in Division One.
What are we living for?
To see Man United in Division Four."

5

In the Shadow of Stretford

I am not one of those fans who automatically hate Manchester United. When I was a young lad, you could not help but admire the skill and the charisma of the "Busby Babes" and the ability of Matt Busby and his staff to organise such a brilliant set-up that they hardly ever needed to pay out huge transfer fees. Bobby Charlton, George Best, Duncan Edwards, Dennis Viollet and many other great players cost them not a penny on the transfer market

Resentment towards "Stretford plc" has built up gradually but inexorably over the years with a similar tempo to that which has seen the widening of the gap between the "haves" and the "have nots" in the world of professional football. Some United fans could be accused of arrogance or of being patronising but the majority (of the genuine fans, that is) are like the rest of us – elated when they win – a feeling that they have experienced much more than County fans over the years. And this is the crux of the matter. A County fan goes to work on a Monday morning, say, in early 1972. The previous week-end his team has lost 0-4 at Exeter. His work-mate, a United fan, is in a jovial mood, his team having won splendidly at White Hart Lane. The United fan cannot resist the temptation to have a dig at the County fan. When this scenario is replicated many times during the course of a season, it's not therefore surprising that a half-time score telling the crowd that United are losing is greeted with a huge cheer. Conversely (and I've heard this on good authority from a pal called John Jones who is that rare type of specimen, a United supporter who actually comes from Manchester) when it was announced at Old Trafford that County had beaten Southampton in the league cup quarter final, the news was greeted with a big cheer.

Manchester United have made me feel like crying on two occasions. The first time, even a 5-1 beating of Crewe Alexandra failed to lift my spirits. I am left with an image in my mind's eye as vivid now as it was over 40 years ago. The match officials and the players of Crewe Alexandra and Stockport County stood on the half way line in silence. The crowd was silent. At that moment it started to snow. The snow fell quite gently. The thoughts of everybody were with those who were fighting for their lives in the hospital in Munich.

Some twenty years later, I was to watch my last match at Old Trafford, vowing never to return to the "Theatre of Dreams", where your dreams can be shattered by blatant cheating (or so it seemed at the time). I refer of course to the infamous league cup tie of 30 August 1978, when County, having been drawn at home, wisely, in my opinion, agreed to play at Old Trafford. And play they did. Even when United scored through Joe Jordan after about ten minutes, County amazed everybody with their style of play and the ease with which they were able to deal with any problems United tried to pose. Mike Summerbee and Lou Macari cancelled each other out, kicking each other more than the ball, without Mr. Willis noticing what was going on and a thumping header from Les Bradd cannoned off Paddy Roche's shoulder and on to the bar. Somehow, United went off at half time 1-0 up. The general feeling was, that if County could keep up this standard of play in the second half, then they were in with a chance.

At the start of the second half, County continued to mount attack after attack upon the United goal (and Summerbee and Macari upon each other). It came as no surprise when Stuart Lee was brought down and Alan Thompson coolly tucked away the ensuing penalty. In a United team which included such star performers as Jordan, Macari, the Greenhoff brothers and Martin Buchan, their most effective player was probably Steve Coppell. However, John Rutter, playing probably his finest game for County, was not letting him have a sniff of the ball. Our other full-back, a youngster by the name of Thorpe, was having a similar effect on Ashley Grimes. With little or no service from the flanks and with Macari neutralised (possibly even neutered) by Summerbee, Jordan and Jimmy Greenhoff were rendered ineffective. Then the best player on the field, Terry Park decided to emphasise the fact. His superb solo goal brought about one of those moments of magic that only fans of teams in the lower reaches of football's pecking order will understand. They occur about once every ten or twenty years. County were beating United 2-1 and looking all the time as though they would add to the score! The United players were visibly rattled. Their fans were giving them a hard time. County should have increased their lead on several occasions. Derek Loadwick was through with only Roche to beat when he was rugby tackled by Gordon McQueen on the edge of the area. Even referee

Willis couldn't miss that one. Exit McQueen stage left as County fans sang the chorus of the song "Jilted John" by Jilted John, "Gordon is a moron, Gordon is a moron." (Lyrics reproduced without the permission of Jilted John for the benefit of those not old or sad enough to be familiar with seventies' pop culture).

Five minutes to go. It should be 4-1. Then came the incidents which turned the "Theatre of Dreams" into County's worst nightmare. Goalkeeper Mike Rogan booted the ball high into the night sky to land it half way inside United's half. Willis blew his whistle.

"That was never offside! What the hell ...?"

Rogan had, allegedly, carried the ball outside his area. Hand ball. Direct free kick. 2-2.

United, given fresh impetus by this huge stroke of luck, attacked again. Joe Jordan barged into the back of Alan Thompson who, somewhat foolishly, retaliated. Free kick to County. A telling-off or a booking for Thompson. All more or less over.

"Hey," someone said, "the replay will be here because this is our home match officially."

But this was Old Trafford. Jimmy Greenhoff scored from the penalty kick awarded for Jordan's foul on Thompson and possibly changed Stockport County's history for the next ten years. I have no axe to grind with Greenhoff. He was doing his job efficiently. The same did not apply to the referee.

It took me quite a while to get over that match. I don't think I've ever felt so sick. Many a parrot was in robust health compared with the County fans who left Old Trafford that evening. When we eventually lost to Liverpool in 1965 and 1984, it was after two magnificent efforts against all odds – but the results were fair. When we lost 2-1 on aggregate to Middlesborough in the Coca-Cola semi final, it was the end of a glorious run and the bitterness of defeat was tempered by pride in what County had achieved. However, at Old Trafford in 1978, a team that had cost a total of £6,000 had taken on a team of internationals and had outplayed them. They were the better side on the night and deserved what would have been a sensational victory. Four years later, County nearly ceased to exist. It was a long time before I could stop myself from joining in the cheering whenever I heard that United were losing.

6

Flight of The Albatross (1964-65)

"The Liverpool fans bayed for blood
as Henshaw raced across the Anfield mud.
He jumped in the air,
The balloons went "pop".
And he gave a double V sign to the Kop."

The above is an extract read out at the 50th birthday of John "The Albatross" Henshaw much to his embarrassment and the delight of his three sons.

It was 30 January 1965 and league champions Liverpool were about to play the league's 92nd club in the fourth round of the FA Cup. The result was considered to be such a foregone conclusion that Bill Shankly had gone to Cologne to watch Liverpool's forthcoming European Cup opponents, leaving a certain Bob Paisley in charge of the team. I remember John being irritated by the lunchtime edition of the "Liverpool Echo", which was forecasting a score of double figures for the home team. Perhaps that was the reason for his action about half an hour before the kick off when someone said that it would be nice to see a County fan go and pop the red balloons which were drifting about in the penalty area in front of the Kop.

"Anyone who tried that would have to be crazy, an absolute loony. He'd be risking his life."

Suddenly, a loony leapt from the paddock. (We were opposite the main stand and fans were not segregated in those days, of course). Before police, stewards, or anybody else for that matter, realised what was happening, Henshaw had run half the length of the pitch and was busy putting paid to the red balloons to the delight of the County fans and howls of derision from the Kop.

"For God's sake," I thought, "Get back here before they flatten you."

But no. He had to prove Andy Warhol right and, grinning inanely, made his gesture of defiance at the famed bank of spectators who had by now altered the lyrics of their anthem to "You'll never walk again", before moving faster than I've ever seen him move before – or since.

Pre-season chat, 1963-64

As stewards and police attempted vainly to bisect the line in which he was running, only to flounder in his slipstream, the by-now heroic Henshaw made it back to the paddock. Here, he found a safe haven, hidden amongst the multitude of County and Liverpool fans who, to their credit, had seen the funny side of the incident.

"Bloody 'ell," said a scouse accent, "If their forwards are as fast as 'im, they might just give us a game."

They weren't quite that fast but they certainly managed to give Liverpool a game

It may be true to say that County's football at times resembled a cavalry charge – never more so than when John Watt raced down the right wing and blasted a cross into the box. The superb Len White sent a bullet header into the net a split second before he collided with the onrushing Tommy Lawrence and was knocked cold.

The state funeral of Winston Churchill had taken place earlier that day and the fans on the Kop observed a two-minute silence – about twenty minutes later than everyone else.

The goal effectively reduced County's attacking options as Len

County players listen intently to Ken Mulhearn's car radio as the draw is made for the Fourth Round: "Team number 1, Liverpool, will play number 92 . . ."

White played the rest of the game suffering from concussion. Even with this disadvantage, the magnificent Trevor Porteous and his heroic band resisted well into the second half until Gordon Milne's half hit shot squirmed its way through a forest of legs and past the unsighted Ken Mulhearn, a very promising young keeper whom Porteous had signed on a free transfer from ... *Everton*!

We now expected County to crumble but this was not to be. Attacking the Kop end, they forced Liverpool back on to the defensive and had a very reasonable claim for a penalty turned down as Ian Sandiford was tackled simultaneously by two Liverpool defenders. A bit later there was a frantic scramble in the Liverpool goalmouth with Lawrence diving all over the place and defenders clearing three times off the line.

The final whistle went and we felt disappointment (we could have easily won), relief (Mulhearn had made several brilliant saves in the last few minutes as County became tired), and elation. We got back to the car just in time to hear Stuart Hall's inimitable match report as County made the national sporting headlines. Notwithstanding the fact that Liverpool had a comfortable 2-0 win in the replay, this was Stockport County's (and Henshaw's) finest hour.

1964-65 was the first season, of several that County had to apply for re-election to Division 4. In the previous couple of seasons there had been rumblings about shortages of cash. The 1963-64 season had begun with great optimism and the team being dubbed "The White Tornadoes" after a 4-0 demolition of Lincoln City. Unfortunately, the Tornadoes failed to batter Doncaster Rovers who were 3-1 winners in the next match at Edgeley Park and, lasting not as long as the instrumental chart toppers of the same name, provided us with a season of mediocrity.

Reg Flewin left and Trevor Porteous was made player-manager. With no money at all to spend, he was forced to scour the list of free transfer players and the reserve teams of other clubs for promising youngsters who might have become available. It was therefore a fairly hotch-potch outfit that turned out for the first game of the season against Millwall. I can remember four things about this match.

* County were awful.
* They lost 4-1.
* Someone in the crowd played "The Last Post" on a trumpet.
* Millwall's goalkeeper was Alex Stepney who was to go on and achieve great fame as the landlord of the Navigation at the top of Lancashire Hill.

County suffered defeat after defeat. Fortunately for me, I was living in Sheffield at the time and missed quite a few of these performances. Eventually, Trevor Porteous was given a bit of money to spend and signed Frank Beaumont from Bury in an attempt to add a bit more experience to what was mainly a team consisting of young players from other clubs' reserves.

However, the FA Cup was to prove to be the making of 1964-65. In the first round we were drawn against Wigan Athletic, then top of the Cheshire League and considered by many to be the best non-league team in the country. Without a doubt, Wigan were favourites to win and it looked very much as though this would be the case as they led 1-0 with County down to ten fit men, with Porteous injured and playing up front. However, when Derek Hodgkinson was brought down in the area, County were given a lifeline as Mike "Ice Cool" Eckersall equalised from the spot. Then, with a replay looking likely and time

Chairman Victor Bernard, the man who brought Friday night football to Edgeley Park

running out, the hobbling Porteous touched the ball to Beaumont who crashed a shot against the underside of the bar. John Nibloe dived bravely to head the ball into the net and County into the second round.

Grimsby Town, the leaders of Division 3, were to be the next visitors to Edgeley Park, but tragically, John Nibloe was to take no further part in the FA Cup. Not realising that he lived in Sheffield, I was shocked to read in the paper that he had been killed in a car crash on the Woodhead Pass, returning to his home after an away match at Newport.

I came over to Stockport to see the first attempt to beat Grimsby but the match was abandoned after 50 minutes due to a combination of fog and a waterlogged pitch. I had to return to Sheffield the next day and my finances did not stretch to another trip to see the second match. However, I was delighted to learn that a goal by Derek Hodgkinson had been enough to earn County a trip to Bristol Rovers who, by the time the third round was staged , had taken over from Grimsby at the top of Division 3.

As a student, I couldn't afford the lengthy trip to Bristol but was once again very pleasantly surprised to learn that County had done more than just hold out for a 0-0 draw and, by all accounts, should have settled matters there and then. The fact that they didn't led to what was apparently one of the most exciting matches ever staged at Edgeley Park. I say "apparently" because I missed it. I offer no excuses or apologies for missing the match. I did what I did, faced with the most awkward dilemma that my nineteen years on this planet could ever have thrown at me.

In the middle of the sixties, with Beatlemania sweeping the nation, I was stuck in a 1958 time warp. My spotty countenance not enhanced by the fact that I looked like a watered-down teddy boy (indeed, I was once nearly beaten up by some Mods and then actually beaten up by some Rockers during the course of a single evening). The reasons for my missing the Bristol match were:

* I had to return to Sheffield to resume my studies.
* I had a ticket for a Chuck Berry concert and the chance to interview the great man for the University newspaper.

It's not every day that you get to interview a Rock 'n Roll legend and it's not every day that County are involved in a third round replay. In fact, little did I realise it at the time but it would be another eight years before I would see County play again at this stage of the competition. I made up my mind and took all the "stick" and scorn that my pals heaped upon me. The interview with Chuck Berry went really well. Recently released from prison, he had become a cult figure and was enjoying to the full the resurrection of his career and gave me the impression that he thoroughly enjoyed performing on stage, particularly when he had a decent backing group. However, it wasn't just Chuck Berry who was "Reelin' and Rockin'" – I had just learned that County had won 3-2!

And so to Anfield. After my desertion over the third round replay, the bubonic plague wouldn't have kept me away from that match. County's league form, with morale no doubt boosted by the FA Cup performances had shown some improvement in December. However, three defeats in which they failed to score preceded the fourth round tie. It was during this poor run of form that Trevor Porteous effected one of County's best ever signings – Len White cost County the princely sum of £1,500 from Huddersfield Town. In one second of skill and courage, Len was to score one of County's most significant goals, get himself knocked flat and repay the club's investment several times over. The replay was something of an anti-climax as Liverpool ran out comfortable winners and went on to win the cup.

County's league form improved – self-belief was probably the main absent factor at the start of the season – but they were too far adrift for improvement to save them from bottom spot. Prior to the match at Liverpool, their league record was: Won 4, Drawn 4, Lost 20, Points 12. Trevor Porteous played his last game for County in a 1-0 home defeat at the hands of Notts County – not a very distinguished conclusion to the career of a man who had given his all to the cause and who could certainly have played at a higher level.

Len White played for most of the following season and, in his all too brief stay at Edgeley Park, averaged a goal every other game. Already at the veteran stage when he joined County, he was subsequently "pensioned off" to Altrincham on a free transfer. This was after the position of Trevor Porteous had been made untenable. I was so annoyed at the treatment these two men had received that I stayed away from the next two home matches in protest.

7

When Friday Night Was County Night – Part 1

As we approached the millennium, there seemed to be a move towards nostalgia for the 1970s – not so if you supported Stockport County FC through that decade and witnessed some of the direst football this side of Benghazi.

I have already whinged at some length about how the decade began and the sorry ending to the 1969-70 season. In fact, the decade began with a 4-1 pasting at Bury and tended to go downhill from there.

County began 1970-71in Division 4 of course and were to have their second most successful season of the decade, reaching the dizzy heights of 11th place. I can remember John Griffiths making a somewhat inauspicious start to his career at Edgeley Park, being carried off in his debut against Peterborough with an injury which looked serious but fortunately wasn't; and being sent off a few days later in a league cup match against Preston for kicking Archie Gemmill.

With the exception of the departed Freddie Goodwin, County had been able to keep their better players and, with the acquisition of Griffiths, Jim Mulvaney and the superb Sammy McMillan, they were able, for the most part, to give as good as they got in this division. However, an ignominious cup exit at the hands of Grantham was to be the first of several capitulations to supposedly inferior opponents over a spell of nearly twenty years.

A major plus was the fact that County managed to discover a young player of considerable promise. Paul Hart proved his worth beyond all conceivable doubt before being transferred to Blackpool, then in Division 2, for a bargain fee of £30,000. He was to spend much of his career in the top flight before returning to haunt us as manager of the Chesterfield team that inflicted upon us the biggest ever aggregate drubbing (6-0) in the 1990 play-offs.

On the downside, Alan Ogley missed most of the season through injury and the team showed that, on occasions, they were capable of the most abject surrender, conceding five goals at Peterborough (when Ogley was injured), Notts County and Aldershot. I can recall one particularly dreadful display – 0-3 at home to Exeter, whose centre-forward, Fred Binney, was very impressive. Gerry McEvoy told me that County were once on the point of signing Binney but his wife didn't fancy coming to live in this area. Why anyone would not want to leave Devon to come and live in sunny Stockport, only Mrs Binney will know!

It was also during this season that County fans had to pay more than any other fans in the country for the dubious privilege of watching fourth division football. Yes, you had to pay more to watch County than to watch Manchester United or Liverpool, or even the league champions – Manchester City! Faced with yet more cash flow problems, the directors had made the decision to increase admission prices to the popular side to ten shillings (50p).

Proof that I am a serial idiot is in a photograph taken at the time. The lone figure disappearing through a turnstile at the Labour Club end of Hardcastle Road, complete with a full head of hair and sideburns is most definitely ... me.

If 1970-71 was not too bad, then 1971-72 vies with 1969-70 as being the nadir of County watching. Fortunately, I was living away from Stockport at that time and so missed out on some of the lowlights of this particular campaign. However, I did witness another thrashing, 0-4 this time, at the hands of Exeter and Fred Binney (has his wife never seen a sunset over Portwood Gasworks?) and three execrable performances over Easter. I must have been suffering from County withdrawal symptoms because I joined about twenty other County fans in witnessing a 5-0 hammering at Hartlepool on Good Friday, a 1-0 defeat at Southport on the Saturday, before rounding off a weekend of unparalleled masochistic bliss by watching a 2-0 defeat at home to Grimsby.

County managed to reach the second round of the FA Cup, having played surprisingly well to win 2-1 at Doncaster, but this was offset by the "Grantham Syndrome" and a 1-0 defeat at Blyth Spartans which resulted in manager Matt Woods receiving his P45 just in time for Christmas.

Brian Doyle became County's umpteenth post war manager but could do little to improve matters in his first half season in charge. County won only four of their last twenty-five games between New Year and the end of the season. I was unable to get to any of these victories and hadn't seen them win since mid-October.

As this was only the second time that County had to apply for re-election to the Football League, they were duly voted back in. Unfortunately for Barrow, they were replaced by cup giant killers Hereford, and consigned to a non-league obscurity that has lasted for over twenty-five years.

However, the prognosis for Stockport County in the summer of 1972 was hardly much better. Brian Doyle, with no money to spend, cobbled together a motley collection of experienced professionals and young unknowns who, for a while at least, were to prove themselves to be something of a surprise package.

Few of the 1971-72 squad remained, most having been scattered to the four winds of non league football – apart from Johnny Price who had become yet another bargain fee departure to Blackburn, the money having been used either to pay wages or to pay debts. County still had experienced players in Ogley, Griffiths, Lawther and Ryden, and four promising youngsters in Paul Hart, Les Ormrod, Ken Fogarty and Ray Charter. Experience was added in the personae of Ingle, Ashworth, Russell, Davidson Tommy Spratt, who was made Captain having come from Doyle's previous club, Workington, and former Barrow player, Eddie Garbett, whose official transfer was "The Football League to Stockport County".

County opened with a 3-2 victory over Peterborough, two of the goals coming from the new captain who, for this season only proved to be very popular with the fans. (Loss of form the following season was to result in his receiving a lot of unfair abuse – some people have short memories.)

Much better progress was made in the league, although the run in the League Cup was to cause poor league form in October. However, this is understandable with such a small squad of players. In the first round of the League Cup, County managed to dispose of Bradford City 2-0 at the third attempt at Burnden Park, a result which, although very welcome was probably quite insignificant compared with what had just happened at the Olympic Games. County's reward for a hard-earned victory was an away tie at First Division Crystal Palace. A goal by Hugh Ryden earned County a well-deserved victory (they even allowed themselves the luxury of a missed penalty); and a home tie with Ron Greenwood's West Ham. And so, on 4 October 1972, I was one of over 13,000 fans crammed into the crumbling stadium known as Edgeley Park.

Sadly, in the not-too-distant future, both Joe Ashworth and Malcolm Russell would receive career-terminating injuries, but not before they had both played significant roles in overcoming the star-studded Hammers. The game was a mere ten minutes old when Russell gave County the lead with an excellent shot from 20 yards. Another ten minutes or so elapsed before another moment of high drama – Eddie Garbett crossed from the right towards the far post. As Ryden was about to head the ball towards goal, he was fouled, obviously and inexplicably by West Ham's right-back, McDowell. No doubt about the penalty – but who would take it? Garbett had scored from the spot at Burnden. Ian Lawther had missed the penalty at Selhurst Park. The referee stood in amazement as nobody came forward to take the penalty. Cometh the moment, cometh the target for next seasons barracking. Spratt strode forward and belted the ball into the roof of the net. God knows what 1973-74 would have been like for him if he had missed. Absolute pandemonium ensued. Twenty minutes gone and County leading 2-0!

Sheer guts, effort and determination are not enough, however, when you are up against one of the best teams in the country – unless, of course, that team happens to be West Ham. Bryan "Pop" Robson pulled one back for the Hammers and was then very unlucky to see another effort rebound off the post into the grateful arms of Alan Ogley. Suddenly, it was half-time. It seemed as though the half had lasted just a couple of minutes!

The second half seemed to last about six hours! County were defending the goal at the Railway End and West Ham laid such a constant siege that, on the rare occasions that the ball ended up in the Cheadle End half of the pitch, roars of approval swept the terraces. On one occasion, County full-back, Steve Ingle won a tackle just outside the penalty area. With nobody in front of him to pass to, he ran about forty yards with the ball before running it into touch and collapsing with exhaustion. He received a great ovation for this effort which was the nearest County got to the West Ham goal in that second half.

As the match entered its final third, the scene was set for Alan Ogley to become the key figure. With players of the calibre of Bobby Moore, Bonds, Lampard, Brooking, Robson, Tyler (signed from the giant-killing Hereford team and about to receive a taste of his own medicine) and the excellent Clyde Best, West Ham were always going to keep Ogley very busy and the brave Yorkshireman spent most of the second half keeping out goalbound shots and headers with every part of his anatomy. Then … with only minutes remaining, a fearful scramble in the goalmouth: about half a dozen County players on the goal line, a shot is scrambled to semi-safety; Ogley dives amid the flying boots, the ball lands on the roof of the net … Corner! Ogley lies injured and West Ham protest at the time taken to administer to the stricken keeper; Ogley back on his feet (or rather foot) obviously in a lot of discomfort; waves of anxiety from the terraces … Corner cleared! Can they hold out? If there's a replay, West Ham will score ten. Charter wins another tackle … Pass it to me Ray … I'm sat in Row L. Then Charter has a brainwave: "The goalie is still allowed to pick up a back pass. They won't amend the rules for several years yet. I'll pass it back to Alan and he can waste a few more seconds – oops! I've gone and passed it to Clyde Best!"

As the awesome Bermudan cut in at speed from the left, the injured keeper hopped towards him to try and narrow the angle and, almost losing his balance, seemed to list to the right. Best unleashed a shot of tremendous power to the keeper's left, bound for the top corner of the net. Somehow propelling himself from the ground with his good leg, Ogley twisted in mid air and got the touch to divert the ball round the post before collapsing once more in an agonised heap. I can't remember how West Ham's fortieth corner was cleared but the ball was quickly returned to the danger area.

It was now the turn of the referee and linesmen to attract the attention of the County faithful, with their impartiality, competence and lineage being described as debatable at best, until the final blast of the whistle was drowned in a thunderous roar. In my mind's eye, I can see the injured Ogley being helped from the field by Clyde Best – a thoroughly decent gesture by a great player and obviously a person of some character.

The night was to yield yet one more hero. David Booth, on arriving first at the pub and mindful of the fact that the pubs used to shut at 10.30 on weekdays, had bought several pints and was placing them on a small round table just as the rest of us arrived.

"You splendid fellow!" I exclaimed, looking greedily at the pints of Robbie's.

"You can bugger off," he replied. "Those are all for me."

And so to Round 4 and a home tie against Norwich City. Now, Why was John Henshaw known as "The Albatross"? At that time, he lived and worked in Malawi and, inspired by County's League Cup exploits, he decided to leave the warmth of East Africa for a holiday in Stockport in November. "The bird of ill omen" duly flew in and was on time to witness the 5-1 drubbing as County's luck finally ran out.

He was off the scene by the time County played Hull City in the third round of the FA Cup. We didn't need any harbinger of doom to make us lose this one, although the then second division side needed a replay to complete the job. The 0-0 draw at Edgeley Park was one of the most distasteful matches I have ever seen. At the moment Hull City are in the lower reaches of Division 3 and I can empathise with all their genuine fans. However, in those days, they had a large following amongst whom was a sizeable group of sub-neanderthalic morons clad in half-mast trousers and "bovver" boots. On witnessing their stampede down Hardcastle Road, I didn't know whether to laugh or crap myself. In those halcyon days of intermingling of fans, they were able to stage quite a sideshow – every time play was held up you could just tune in to the fights on the pop side.

The match was "refereed" by Hull player-manager, Terry Neill, the ex-Arsenal and Northern Ireland international. Ian Lawther was sent off for retaliation but was saved from suspension by the impartial testimony of a vicar from Chesterfield who just happened to be at the match. What he was doing there, I have no idea. However, Lawther must have been grateful for his attendance and the vicar would have been able to collect enough material for several sermons.

Hull had a full-back called Bardsley whose sole intention appeared to be to commit GBH upon anyone wearing a white shirt. Unbelievably, he was not even booked. I just wish that this guy could have had the chance to play against Diego Maradona. He made Andoni Goicoechea look like Gary Lineker.

After their exploits in both cup competitions, County were in with an outside chance of promotion until about the end of March. Overall it was a decent season, particularly since they had a good reserve team which, under the guidance of Jim Mulvaney, won the Lancashire League. Ironically, County were to have quite a say as to which club took the last promotion place – ironically because it would go to either Newport County or Aldershot (r.i.p both of them). In their last two home games, County beat Newport 1-0, and, with the crowd boosted by many Aldershot fans and even some from Newport willing Stockport County to win, drew 1-1 with the Hampshire club, thus allowing them the point they needed to clinch promotion. Jubilant Aldershot fans celebrated all over Edgeley Park.

8

When Friday Night Was County Night – Part 2

In his first full season in charge, Brian Doyle had done a fine job and the outlook for 1973-74 was quite optimistic. Although Paul Hart had gone on to better things, County still had some useful players and, at last it would appear, some confidence on which to build. It was not to be. The season began rather strangely – Played 10, Won 1, Drawn 8, Lost 1 – the only defeat being a 0-4 reverse at Barnsley where County were completely outplayed under the approving gaze of Test Cricket Umpire Dickie Bird. A few beers were needed to help me get over that one, but was history going to repeat itself?

County had beaten Port Vale 2-0 in the first round of the League Cup (a very good performance) and were drawn once again against Crystal Palace, this time at home. The previous September Palace had been riding high in the First Division but, probably due to the shock of losing to County, had nosedived down the table so badly that they were eventually relegated. Now, under the guidance of Malcolm Allison, they were looking to repeat the performance.

Allison had spent a lot of money assembling a team of so-called star players. However, at the end of 90 minutes, the biggest surprise was that County only won 1-0. About three weeks earlier, Brian Doyle had signed a somewhat inconsistent winger from Scunthorpe, called Harry Kirk. On his debut, Kirk had run the Mansfield right full back ragged, but had followed this display with two or three stinkers just to let us know what to expect. On his day, or in this case night, Harry could be quite brilliant. He was up against Paddy Mulligan, the Republic of Ireland international whom Allison had signed from West Brom. In a dazzling performance of wing play, Kirk treated us to every trick in the book and a few more besides. At half time the dizzy Mulligan was taken off to be replaced by former Chelsea and Scotland star, Charlie Cooke. The woodwork, poor finishing and a superb display by John Jackson in the Palace goal were the main reasons why only full back Ray Charter was able to find the net. Charlie Cooke left the field in a similar condition to Mulligan as Harry Kirk left us wondering how it was possible for a player to be so brilliant in one match and so hopeless in the next. The reward for this victory was another cup tie against Hull City, this time at Boothferry Park. It was too far to go for a midweek game and, in any case, I wanted to carry on living. I was glad I didn't go – Hull won 4-1.

Worse was to come. County only managed seven league wins in the entire season, although Mick Hollis scored a creditable 15 goals in 39 matches. It was even rumoured at one stage that Tommy Docherty was interested in signing him, as he masterminded United's demise into Division 2. And, of course, Brian Doyle paid the usual price for seeing his team finish bottom of the Football League.

As Labour won the General Election that spring, I could not help comparing Edward Heath's administration with Stockport County – promised much, achieved nothing and caused us all a lot of grief. There was one slight difference. County managed to get re-elected. Throughout this decade, being a Stockport County supporter was not an easy task. I could stand the jibes and the scorn from work colleagues but when United and City fans actually expressed *sympathy*, that was just too much! Perhaps the sympathy expressed by United fans stemmed from the fact that they too had experienced the bitter taste of failure. With the emergence of several high profile non league clubs (Altrincham could have wiped the floor with County in those days), re-election to the Football League was by no means a foregone conclusion. Even though the weather was often foul in June, County fans spent quite a few sweaty early summers praying that the axe would not fall.

As the country recalled former Prime Minister Harold Wilson, so County recalled former manager Jimmy Meadows to see if he could bring about an improvement in the club's position. This he duly did. A 0-0 draw at Scunthorpe on the last day of the season meant that County finished fifth from the bottom. Oh! The sweet taste of success! The highlights of 1974-75? Were there any? The best performances were the 3-2 home win over Mansfield Town and a 1-1 draw in the return match at Field Mill before 10,000 fans. Why so many? Because, in spite of those two results, Mansfield won promotion. I resisted the urge to go to Field Mill because I had been there the season before to witness the 5-0 trouncing that the home team handed out. A 3-0 home defeat by Barnsley on Boxing Day just about ruined Christmas, coming as it did just a few weeks after the "Grantham Syndrome" had struck once more. This time it was Stafford Rangers who inflicted the torture. However, County did manage to hold them to a 0-0 draw at Edgeley Park before losing the replay 1-0. Oh yes, and we also managed to go out of the League Cup at the first attempt, losing 2-0 to Blackburn once again!

Jimmy Meadows had had enough and had resigned (or was he sacked? – I can't remember) and County's new manager was Roy Chapman, father of Lee, and with a highly successful track record at Stafford Rangers. Could this be the man to bring some long awaited much needed success to Edgeley Park? In a word, "no". However, the general feeling amongst the fans was that we had a decent manager who could have done with a bit more support from the board. The summer of 1975 proved to be a glorious one, the sun shining from a powder blue sky as bouncers flew in abundance past the ear lobes of English batsmen who, in the immortal words of their captain, had been going to make the West Indians grovel. And this was a rare summer in that dire decade when County, for once, didn't have to grovel. Twentieth position in Division 4 meant that they would not be starting 1975-76 in non league football, for which the ground, in any case, did not come up to scratch.

The 1975-76 season began with the usual, by now, ominous prognosis. A 0-0 draw at home to Crewe, a League Cup defeat (1-3) in the first leg at Southport, a 1-3 defeat at home to Northampton and 1-2 in the second leg with Southport. County managed to win the odd match here and there as the season wore on, but by the end of November, things were looking rather bleak:

Played 17, Won 4, Drawn 4, Lost 9, Points 12

And one of the bottom four positions apparently reserved permanently for Stockport County.

In spite of this state of affairs, Dave Booth and myself had enjoyed the trip to Bradford and County's fluke 2-1 win. In those days of non segregation, fans viewing the match from the side would usually gravitate towards the end which their team was attacking in the hope of getting a better view of the ensuing goals.

It was more in hope than anticipation, therefore, that Dave and I took up a position of semi-isolation level with the penalty spot in front of the Bradford goal. I can't recollect seeing many other County fans at that particular game but there must have been some there.

Bradford were leading 1-0 when their goalkeeper, Peter Downsborough, misjudged a cross and Lee Bradley equalised. It was not a happy afternoon for the unfortunate goalkeeper who, shortly afterwards, and with the ball at the other end of the field, clobbered Steve Massey. It was at this point (Dave and I liked to think so, anyway), that we secured a County victory by drawing the attention of a fairly somnolent linesman to this piece of no doubt reciprocated skulduggery. The referee awarded a penalty which was competently dispatched by Massey himself.

I think it was Ernest Hemingway who put forward the idea that one day should be set aside each year when you could murder with impunity people whom you detested. If such a weird notion ever should ever come to fruition, I would spend that day as far away from Downsborough as possible.

The best thing about the FA Cup that year was the fact that County avoided humiliation at the hands of a non-league club. They managed this courtesy of a 3-0 drubbing in the first round at Hartlepool.

Enter George Best.

Improved form in the new year saw County achieve (almost) mid-table mediocrity and, with six games remaining, had amassed 36 points at a time when 40 points was deemed to be the safety figure. Even a 5-0 walloping at Swansea was not enough to suggest that County would have to apply for re-election. However, their performance in match number 41 was. The defeat was only 3-1 but Crewe were pretty dire as well. It really was a dreadful match. County's goal was a penalty scored by Wyn Davies,the former Welsh international who had played with distinction at City, United and Newcastle – "sic transit gloria mundi". For readers unfamiliar with Latin, the phrase means "Gloria Mundy has been sick in the minibus", probably on the way home from watching County lose at Crewe.

The performance at Gresty Road was so putrid that Boothy, McEvoy and myself, homeward bound from this debacle and on considering the remaining fixtures, were now in some trepidation as regards the spectre of re-election. It was with elation, therefore that I learned of the 3-2 mid-week victory over Rochdale. (Would I have gone if I hadn't been working? Indeed, was I working?). County now had 38 points and needed only two more to ensure safety.

Poor deluded fools that football supporters are! Not only did County fail to get a single point from their last five games, they also failed to score – in order to do that you have to place a shot or a header in the general direction of your opponents' goal. As we slouched despondently away from the last home match (v Tranmere, 0-2), it was apparent that only victory in the last match at promoted Northampton would prevent County from having to apply for re-election for the third time in five seasons. Northampton duly administered the "coup de grace" with a 4-0 thrashing.

It goes without saying that Roy Chapman parted company with the club that had lured him away from his successful reign at Stafford. It had now become a ritual amongst us to arrange a night out in June to either celebrate re-election to the Football League or possibly also to drown our sorrows. We were in luck once again and able to enjoy the glorious summer of 1976, secure in the knowledge that we still had a team to support.

The new manager was Eddie Quigley, back for his second spell in charge. For a while, it looked as though he was going to achieve the same success as he had done ten years earlier. Although this was not to be, 1976-77 proved to be a much better season and County went on to allow their fans the unaccustomed luxury of seeing their team finish in a respectable mid-table position.

In a splendid start to the season, we were also treated to a decent run in the League Cup. Throughout August, County's new centre forward, Barney Daniels, signed on a free transfer from City, looked as though he intended to break the club's goalscoring record before Christmas and the perfomances of Steve Massey were attracting a lot of attention from the bigger clubs.

By the end of August, County found themselves at the top of the league and in the second round of the League Cup. They were drawn away at second division Blackburn. Steve Massey highlighted a brilliant individual performance by scoring twice in the 3-1 win.

This set up a home tie against Everton and County's biggest crowd for four years saw them lose a hard-fought game 0-1, their first defeat of the season. From then on, things went slightly downhill.

County v Everton, 10 September 1976.
County's Steve Massey and Everton's Dave Jones pause for thought.
Massey: "I wonder how many first division managers are watching me from that stand?"
Jones: "I'd hate to end up working in a dump like this."

9

Wembley Blues

The expressions "Stockport County" and "Wembley" used never to occur in the same sentence. Like two parallel lines, they would never meet. That is, until the football authorities moved the winning post and made it possible for fans of all 92 league clubs to have a more realistic dream of being able to walk down Wembley Way, buy a rancid hot dog for about £2, submit to a search before entering the stadium, buy a lukewarm pint of toxic waste for £3 and a programme for £5. It's not every day that your team gets to Wembley, is it? And, in the case of County fans, see your team play badly and lose to the likes of Stoke, Peterborough, Port Vale and Burnley.

Whatever those people who supported County through the desperate years between 1969 and 1989 may think of Dragan Lukic, it has to be admitted that it was his idea and perseverance which led to the implementation of the competition originally known as the Freight Rover Trophy.

Until the arrival of Brendan Ellwood, the people he brought in to run the club and the appointment of Danny Bergara, County had the unenviable record of failing to win a single match in this competition. However, in 1991-92, the law of averages applied and County made up for previous failure by going all the way and ended up playing Stoke City in the third 'X' rated fixture between the clubs in the space of a week.

Danny Bergara's dream was about to come true. He was to become the first South American to lead out an English club side at Wembley, just beating Ossie Ardiles to it. It proved to be a great occasion in spite of the defeat in a tight and, at times, unpleasant match. This was the first episode in the saga of "Danny Bergara's nearly men". The most memorable moment for me was when County's "goal" was disallowed after about four minutes. Darren Knowles ran down the right and slung over a high centre. Stoke goalkeeper, Peter Fox, and Paul Wheeler jumped for the ball. Both of them missed it and it landed in the back of the net. We were right behind that goal and rose as one to acclaim our taking the lead. To the derision of the Stoke fans to our right, we sat down as one, as the goal was disallowed. All of us, that is except one – a young gentleman who turned his back to the Stoke fans, dropped his trousers and "mooned" at them. Taking umbrage at this "cheeky" display, stewards removed the young man from the stadium – a 400-mile round trip for about four minutes of football. Still, at least he saw the best part of the match.

Another memory of that day was seeing Jimmy Hill outside the stadium, surrounded by County fans who were not slow to remind him that we had done the double over Fulham. To his credit, Hill was very pleasant and friendly to the fans and signed loads of autographs for the kids. (Jim – the pen you used was not a biro but one of those felt type things. Your signature rubbed off the glossy page of my programme!)

Quiz time: What have Stockport County and the Swiss national side of 1996 got in common?

Answer: They are the only two teams ever to have lost twice at Wembley in the space of eight days.

If Stoke's Autoglass win was a Pyrrhic victory, then County' play-off triumph over them was mega-Pyrrhic. Enter Peterborough United, Ken Charlery and Martin Bodenham. Since that fateful afternoon, Both Charlery and Bodenham have taken quite a lot of stick from County fans. In the case of Charlery, the reception that he used to receive on ensuing visits to Edgeley Park was a sort of back handed compliment. Even when he later became a County player, he was not very popular with the fans. On that warm May afternoon, both Bodenham and Charlery did their jobs in honest fashion, the latter very competently, the former, in my opinion, somewhat less than competently.

Fred Barber, he of the strange mask, was keeping goal for Peterborough that day, and he did his best to see County right by palming a cross right on to the head of Kevin Francis. Ironically, Barber was in goal for Chesterfield a year later when, guilty himself of blatant time wasting, was much aggrieved at Paul Williams' inability to follow protocol (a la Kanu) with a throw-in which led to a corner, which led to a goal from Kevin Francis. The outcome of this dubious victory was another trip to Wembley and another three match rubber against a side from the Potteries.

It was not a good time to lose form and, although County made it hard for Port Vale, particularly in the 1-1 draw at Edgeley and the second half of the Autoglass final, there was no doubt that Port Vale were the better side during the course of those eight days. Well, there's always next year.

One of the best aspects of Danny Bergara's reign was the fact that, after failure in the play-offs, he always seemed to be able to motivate the players for the following season. In most cases, teams that lose in the play-offs seem to do badly the following season. This was never the case with Danny and his teams.

1989-90 – Division 4 – 4th – Lost to Chesterfield (SF)

1990-91 – Division 4 – 2nd – Automatic promotion.

1991-92 – Division 3 – 5th – Lost to Peterborough (F)

1992-93 – Division 2 – 6th – Lost to Port Vale (SF)

1993-94 – Division 2 – 4th – Lost to Burnley (F)

Watching County over that five-year period, heartache aside, was for the most part very entertaining. They won most of their games, played some exciting football and scored a lot of goals. However, the bubble really burst on that Sunday afternoon when they met arch-rivals Burnley. Perhaps "fired up" too much, they really shot themselves in the collective foot. Much has been written about that match, so all I will say is that this was by far the worst of my four Wembley experiences.

10

Favourite Goals

After the awful recollections of Wembley, I am now going to indulge myself. As a County fan for over 40 years, I am going to select the 12 most memorable goals I have seen just to cheer myself up. Probably the best goal in terms of individual skill scored by a County player was a magnificent effort by Steve Massey in a 1-1 draw with Doncaster Rovers some time in the late 1970s. I make no apologies for not including that one because I have based my choice on the "feel good" factor engendered by these goals rather than the actual quality. Unfortunately, Massey's moment of magic was witnessed by a sparse crowd in the days before matches were either televised or videoed. But I am sure that the 1500 or so who were there will remember him beating five defenders in a very limited amount of space before curling a shot around the advancing goalkeeper.

I shall endeavour to keep readers in suspense by announcing my choices in reverse order.

Number 12: Andy Preece. County 2, Darlington 0. 18 January 1992.

A miserable, wet, freezing afternoon was the setting for this particular masterpiece. Quite rightly, Andy Preece will be best remembered by County fans for his winner in the cup-tie against Queens Park Rangers. However, this effort brightened up what was otherwise a fairly drab 90 minutes. County were leading 1-0 through Peter Ward and, with about 20 minutes remaining, were not convincing us fully of their ability to hold out for the three points. Suddenly, Preece found himself running on to a through ball into the penalty area with the whole goal to aim at and only the keeper to beat. The chance had seemingly come from nowhere and Darlington goalkeeper, Prudhoe, was as surprised as Preece at the swiftness with which the situation had developed. Prudhoe failed to advance quickly enough to narrow the angle but Preece shot straight at him, the ball going straight through his legs into the net!

Number 11: Levi Edwards. County 2, Cardiff City 0. 22 November 1986.

I was fortunate enough not to witness what was arguably County's worst ever performance, namely the 0-1 defeat at Caernarfon Town, at the time when Colin Murphy had just returned from the Saudi Arabia to take over the side which Jimmy Melia had been grooming for oblivion. The Caernarfon match was Murphy's first back in charge and he must have wished he was still in the desert. From what I could gather, eleven camels would have done better. Murphy had had just one week to try to instil some backbone into the lamentable team he had inherited. The Cardiff fans had been in great spirits, reminding the home supporters of the ignominy suffered the previous week at the hands of their fellow countrymen. However, Murphy gave notice of what was to come as County held on grimly to the early lead given them by Vernon Allatt. Promotion chasing Cardiff were pressing for the equaliser but County broke from defence and Edwards blasted the ball into the net with about four minutes left for play. It isn't that the goal was all that memorable. It was more the reaction that it produced. With the town centre full of Christmas shoppers, County had won at home for the first time that season. Edwards raced around the side of the pitch as though he had just scored the winning goal in the World Cup final and we roared our heads off in a mixture of relief and ecstacy.

Number 10: Oshor Williams. County 2, West Brom 3. August 1980.

This was a pre-season friendly, with 4th Division County taking on a West Brom side then in the 1st Division. With the Baggies perhaps not playing as though their lives depended on the result, County were playing quite well and were only trailing 2-1, when a cross from the right found Tony Coyle at the corner of the six yard box. In his haste to get on to the score sheet, Coyle blasted the ball first time. Unfortunately for him and for West Brom too, as it turned out, the ball went like a rocket back in the direction from whence it had come, smacked Oshor on the forehead and went flying into the top of the net. John Osborne in the West Brom goal, and his defenders just shrugged their shoulders. How can you defend against a move like that?

Number 9: Alun Armstrong. County 2, Everton 3. 17 January 1996.

What a goal! Seconds remaining and Alun outwitted two Everton defenders and crashed home the equaliser. Henshaw and McEvoy jumped up and down hugging each other with delight. Henshaw knackered his back and watched in agony, both literally and figuratively, as Everton took the kick off, went straight down the field and scored the winner.

Number 8: Andy Mutch. Southampton 1, County 2. 29 January 1997.

Perhaps the superb diving header by Luis Cavaco in the first match at Edgeley Park should be given pride of place over what was a simple tap in and a goal which we witnessed on television rather than "live". Having been down to Birmingham to visit the Lawnmower Man the previous weekend, we offer no excuses for not going down to the south coast for a mid-week match, preferring instead to descend upon the satellite owning David "Bring your own beer" Thompson. The fact that everybody did as he suggested meant that the plumbing facilities in the Thompson household took a bit of a bashing at half-time. In the second half, as the game became very exciting, beer was being consumed at the same frantic tempo as the game was being played. McEvoy could hold on no longer. As the ball went out for a throw-in, he dashed off to use the facilities. Apparently he was just on the point of blessed relief when a roar from the lounge told him that something very significant had happened. It's a good job that Mutch's aim was better than that of McEvoy. Our damp-trousered companion made it back to the TV set just in time to witness the action replay. Remembering Everton, Henshaw laughed so much that his trousers nearly met with the same fate

Number 7: Ian Dowie. County 2, West Ham 1. 18 December 1996.

Ian Dowie is a good professional footballer who has spent most of his career in the top flight and has represented Northern Ireland on many occasions. I state the obvious to counterbalance the fact that Dowie perpetrated probably the biggest blooper by an opposing player that I have ever seen. Brett Angell's header from Tom Bennett's cross was a good enough goal but the County striker would have been prouder still if he, instead of Dowie, had managed to get on the end of Mike Flynn's cross and score with such a precise and powerful header. Flynn, out on the right, retrieved the ball after his long throw-in had been only partially cleared. He outwitted a defender and sent over an inviting cross for Dowie to rise majestically above everyone and send an absolute beauty past the flabbergasted Miklosko.

Number 6: John Jeffers. County 2, Carlisle United 0. 26 December 1995.

In spite of the fact that it should not have been played, this match proved to be highly entertaining. The kick off had been delayed whilst ice was removed from the Railway End terracing and a pale winter sun failed to remove frost from most of the pitch. County had taken the lead in the first half with a very good goal, Alun Armstrong running on to an excellent through ball from Ben Thornley to lob the ball cleverly over the advancing keeper. Jeffers' party piece came about half way through the second half. People may get the impression that JJ was a one-footed player, using his right leg just for standing on. (The goal that he scored at Bristol Rovers in the match of the famous cross bar height controversy would seem to contradict that theory), However, the Carlisle defenders seemed to think that if they could force him to play the ball with his right foot, there would be little chance of his achieving anything constructive. The outcome was like a ballet on ice as Jeffers skated past four or five defenders, using his right foot only once – to prod the ball past the advancing keeper to roll it gently into the net. A goal that was worth getting frost bite for.

Number 5: Arnold Jackson. County 3, Luton Town 0. 4 January 1958.

Although nowadays County play in a higher division than Luton, way back in 1958 the southern Hatters were riding high in the First Division and had several internationals in their side. A week before their Third Round trip to Edgeley Park, they had beaten Arsenal 4-0! County were in the middle of the old Third Division North and didn't seem to have much of a chance – that is until the third minute of the match when Arnold's header planted Mike Davock's cross from the left firmly past England goalkeeper, Ron Baynham. The goal was scored at the Cheadle End and I was stood right behind the goal. I thought the place was going to collapse. There was a famous picture which appeared in the "FA Book for Boys" for that season – a snapshot taken as Jackson made contact with the ball and timed in such a way that the ball obscures his face and neck. The caption read: "If you spend enough time with one you start to look like one."

Number 4: Ernie Moss. County 1, Scunthorpe United 0. 13 April 1987.

This is the second goal from a season which could have proved to be the most disastrous one ever. If Levi Edwards' goal against Cardiff pointed the way to salvation, Ernie's superb 25 yard volley finally ensured salvation. Having spent his entire career scoring a lot of goals in the bottom two divisions, Ernie was nearing the end of his career when Colin Murphy signed him from Chesterfield on Christmas Eve 1986. He went on to play a significant role in County's great escape. Having scored most of his goals from well inside the penalty area, Ernie seemed to be more surprised than anybody at the quality of this particular strike.

Number 3: Alun Armstrong. County 3, Manchester City 1. 29 November 1997.

Never mind the tremendous opening goal from Paul Cooke, I have selected this one because of a photograph in the "Football Pink" shows the glum faces of the City fans in the Railway End. Among them are two pals of mine, Ian Armstrong and John Nevins. Sorry lads!

Number 2: Terry Park. County 2, Manchester United 3. 30 August 1978. (Correct result 2-1)

A brilliant individual goal scored in the setting that such a goal deserves.

Number 1: Len White. Liverpool 1 County 1. 30 January 1965.

A goal achieved thanks to the great skill and courage of the perpetrator – the first act in a drama which, for those of us who are old enough to have been there, will always be County's finest hour.

11

Charlie's Penalty and a Dirty Trick

Throughout the fifties, County had always been one of the better teams in the Third Division North. They emphasised this fact by again managing to finish in the top half of the table in 1957-58, finishing in a creditable 9th position by winning three of their last four matches to become members of the newly created Third Division. However, the 1958-59 season was to me the first, and by no means the last, time when being a County fan was not the easiest way to spend a good portion of your leisure time.

And so, as Fidel Castro's guerrilla fighters marched triumphantly into Havana, County marched less than triumphantly into the Fourth Division, where they were to spend 27 of the next 30 years. This relegation was to have a far-reaching effect on the club as a whole. The ensuing slump in attendances meant that there was very little money available for any manager to spend and, although there were one or two promising moments in the early sixties, it was mostly a disappointing time for the fans.

Friday night football had not yet been considered and that meant that I didn't see too many matches since, on most Saturday afternoons my services were required by a fairly dysfunctional outfit known as Dialstone Lane FC. We didn't have any fans at all to moan at us, which was just as well.

However, back to Edgeley Park and one match that I was able to attend was the Monday evening match on 28 August 1961 against Southport. I have just rabbited on at length about some of my favourite goals, but this match stands out because of my favourite missed chance. It had been an uneasy summer with World War III becoming a distinct possibility because of the Cuban missile crisis and the Bay of Pigs fiasco. With the world on the brink of nuclear war, or so it seemed to me at the time, I became even more paranoid as County contrived to lose their first three matches of the season. The last time that they had managed to do that was in 1939!

Hoping for an improved performance, I went along with the, by

The 1961-62 team

now, usual bunch, to the Southport game. It soon became apparent that there would be no such improvement as Southport were 3-0 up before I could convince anyone that the end of the world was nigh. I decided not to bother trying. Watching County was bad enough.

I must digress from the match for a moment. In those days, Gerry McEvoy and Mick Orr were apprentice printers at the "Stockport Advertiser" and, of course, had to suffer the indignities that have been heaped upon apprentices since time immemorial. Gerry had recently been the victim of a rather unpleasant trick when one of his work-mates had generously added bicarbonate of soda to the pint of milk that he was accustomed to drink each morning.

In spite of this, nothing seemed to have dulled the lad's generosity of spirit as he pulled out a packet of Wrigley's spearmint chewing gum and handed everyone a stick with an equanimity that the 0-3 scoreline belied.

As we chewed on the gum, he told us of the revenge he had exacted upon the unsuspecting Linotype Operators of the "Stockport Advertiser". "I went to the chemist's," he said, "and bought some of that laxative chewing gum. Then I got some ordinary Wrigley's and swapped over the wrappers very carefully. They were so surprised at me giving anything away, they all grabbed a piece and shoved it in their gobs."

As one, we all stopped chewing. McEvoy grinned widely at the volley of abuse and the rest of us were much relieved to realise that he had not repeated the trick – opting instead to do a "double take" to see what the reaction would be. Given the rudimentary facilities of Edgeley Park in 1961, it was just as well.

For week after week, that summer, people had been glued to their TV sets, not to catch what was happening in Washington or Moscow, but to see the outcome of the serial "The Fugitive" – not the Harrison Ford/ Tommy Lee Jones version but the equally well done original starring David Janssen and Barry Morse.

"One bloke was so bad," said Gerry, "that he had to miss the last episode of 'The Fugitive'."

"You should have saved some of that gum for the Southport team," said one of the lads, "that way we might have stood a chance."

Our wayward attention was suddenly drawn back to the match as County were awarded a dubious penalty. Now we had the chance to reduce the deficit and mount a glorious fight back. But who would take the kick? Up stepped close season signing from Tranmere, Charlie McDonnell, surely about to open up his goal scoring account. The crowd went silent in the anticipation of seeing the net bulge as Charlie shaped to take the kick. There was a tremendous roar – from the Southport fans as Charlie's first, and last, penalty for Stockport County, cleared the Railway End terracing, nearly taking with it the rickety scoreboard and probably ended up on the 8.05 to London Euston.

"I bet he even missed the last episode of 'The Fugitive'." said Mick.

In defence of Charlie, he proved to be a far better player than this inauspicious beginning seemed to suggest and, indeed, did manage to score later in what turned out to be a 4-1 defeat. He managed to score 16 goals that season as County recovered from their desperate start and finished ninth from the bottom. He scored the same number the following year, averaging almost a goal every other game, before he returned to Tranmere.

As for McEvoy, all I can say is: "With friends like that, who needs enemas?"

And as for Stockport County, friends were becoming fewer and fewer with gates dwindling and financial crisis looming.

12

Raw Deals

There are occasions when the fans of a team have good reason to hurl abuse at their own players. Managers and coaches will usually stand up for the players in public and claim that this attitude is counter-productive. I have already mentioned that I was not very impressed with one or two players the first few times that I saw them in action. However, I was quite pleased to be proved wrong, the manager having shown that his judgement was more reliable than mine. On the other hand, without its fans a club is nothing and what does annoy me is the manager who talks down to the fans and says that they have no right to express an opinion. In the days before fans were segregated, I have heard fans defend the very players they were barracking when those players have been criticised by opposing supporters. "He may be a donkey but he's *our* donkey!"

In my opinion, a player deserves all the calumny he may get if:

* He is simply not trying and is just there to pick up a wage packet.
* He is obviously not good enough and should not be masquerading as a professional footballer. (Those who fall into this category tend to be let off fairly lightly with the manager receiving most of the vituperation for having selected them in the first place).
* He does something so crassly stupid that he jeopardises his team's chances of winning the match,

Everyone who goes regularly to support any team or watches high profile games on TV will be able to think immediately of several examples of all three categories, and so I shall refrain from mentioning examples, either at Edgeley Park or elsewhere.

Unfortunately, over the years, there have been a number of people on both the playing and coaching side at County who have come into none of the above categories, but who have been unjustly subjected to a hail of scorn that has poured down from the terraces, or more recently from the seats.

When I first started watching County, the main target for the fans' displeasure was a winger called Ken Finney. He could play on either wing and occasionally played as a stand-in centre-forward. It is over 40 years since he last played for County – so my memory may not be serving me too well – but as I recall, Finney was not a bad player at all. Maybe it was his name (Proud Preston had the legendary Tom, whereas humble County had Ken).

In any event, it was poor Ken's fate to be berated by the crowd when things were not going well for the team as a whole. One of my first excursions to watch an away match was to the Fourth Round FA cup tie at Upton Park in 1958. I can recall Finney crossing for Bill Holden to give County the lead but, later on, with County losing 3-1, he started to receive some abuse from the fans. If there had been substitutes in those days, he might even have been taken off. However, Finney stuck resolutely to his task and reduced the arrears with a shot-cum-centre to set up a fantastically exciting finish. He played nearly 200 games for County and scored about 40 goals – not bad for a winger who was supposed to be hopeless.

When County crumbled to ignominious defeat at the hands of Caernarfon Town in 1986, a fair percentage of the players that day fell into the first two categories mentioned earlier. There were of course, one or two notable exceptions around whom the returning Colin Murphy built a side which was resilient enough to battle its way out of trouble and avoid becoming the first club to be relegated automatically from the Football League. This was to be the fate of Murphy's former club, Lincoln City, after he had taken them to the threshold of Division 2 a couple of years earlier.

Whenever he has returned to Edgeley Park, Murphy has received a reception which might best be described as vitriolic. The reason for these feelings of resentment, or even hatred, is that not only did he accept Lincoln's request to return there and try to resurrect their fortunes but that he also managed to retrieve league status for them at the first attempt. This was achieved after taking with him from County several of the players who had helped him to perform the miracle of self-preservation of the previous season.

However, without the timely return to Edgeley Park of Colin Murphy, County would have been consigned to oblivion and would most likely have departed the Football League with a record worse than even the 1969-70 performance. Under those hypothetical circumstances, it is doubtful whether Brendan Ellwood would have considered County's cause as being worthy of consideration. I propose a "Be kind to Colin Murphy" week.

It is a fairly strange phenomenon but the players the crowds "get at" seem to be, for the most part, quite decent players. Perhaps their mistakes tend to stand out because they refuse to "hide" during the course of a match if things are not going well. I have already mentioned Tommy Spratt. More recently it has been the fate of Chris Beaumont and Jim Gannon who have borne the brunt of the "ire of Edgeley". Signed by Danny Bergara from Rochdale for a fee of about £8,000, just prior to the Uruguayan's first full season in charge, Beaumont was injured in about his second match for County. He was unable to return until December, only claiming a place for the last third of the season. He played a major role in the drive to the play-off finals and, from March onwards had Jim Gannon to help him share the abuse that rained down from the terraces. The fact that both players were key figures in the promotion season that followed proves that they are both either stone deaf or have sufficient strength of character and self-belief to go on and prove that their detractors were wrong. Both played major roles in getting County to Wembley for the first time. In the second leg of the Autoglass Northern Final against Burnley, Beaumont chased a lost cause, won a corner, took it and Kevin Francis headed home. Gannon scored the second goal to ensure that Danny Bergara's Wembley dream would come true.

13

Fifty Miles Wide

Although I have been a County fan for over forty years, I am not one of the elite band that will travel the length and breadth of the country in support of the cause. No trip to Brighton on New Year's day or Torquay on Boxing Day for me, thank you very much. It was bad enough watching the outcome of those matches on Ceefax. The furthest afield I have travelled to watch the team is London (Wembley and West Ham) and the North East, my last venture to that part of the country being to watch the 4-1 pasting administered to us in the Stadium of Light.

Normally, my away days have been limited to Yorkshire, Lancashire and Derbyshire and, more often than not, in spite of our dreadful record between 1969 and 1989, I have enjoyed most of those trips.

Oakwell

This is a ground that I have visited on several occasions. The match in 1972-73 is one that I remember quite well, probably due to the fact that County won 3-1. As mentioned earlier, this season was an oasis of entertainment in the middle of the desert of dross of 1971-72 and 1973-74. The game took place in January 1973, a week before the vicar from Chesterfield felt moved to speak up for Ian Lawther after that appalling match against Hull City. County were actually in the top half of the table and one of the better players was forward, John Griffiths, whose angelic, choir boy-like appearance belied his actual character. I would imagine that Griffiths was aged about 23 to 25 at that time but looked about 15. As the teams took the field, a voice behind me, with an accent which left no room for doubt as to which team the owner of it supported, proclaimed in amusement:

"Hey look at that little lad they've got playing centre-forward! I thought 'e was t' bloody mascot!"

A few minutes later, the same voice informed all in its vicinity:

"'E's not a bad player, that little lad!"

And about five minutes after that:

"'E's a bloody dirty sod, that little lad!"

With about five minutes of the match remaining, the "little lad" scored County's third and the "voice", now reduced to a mutter, went home.

The following season, Barnsley and the "voice " wreaked ample revenge, the 4-0 walloping being restricted to that margin by a heroic performance (again) by Barnsley born Alan Ogley in the County goal.

Another eventful match at Oakwell was one that I missed. When you have small children, there are times when you have to give your team a miss, especially when they are near the bottom of the Fourth Division. At that time County were doing so badly that I probably wouldn't have gone in any case. As it turned out, I was with my children in Lyme Park, having gone for a walk and then for an hour or so of torture in the Adventure Playground. Gerry McEvoy and his two boys were there and it was from Gerry's car radio that we learned that County were losing 3-0. As the crisp February afternoon turned quite chilly, we managed to persuade the kids that enough was enough and decided to make our way home. We learned from Radio Manchester, as GMR used to be called, that Phil Henson had pulled one back for County but that promotion chasing Barnsley had quickly added a fourth. Unable to stand the torture any longer, Gerry switched to national radio. Every time I listened to a local radio station in those days, the commentary on the United or City match would be interrupted at regular intervals with – "And it's more bad news for Stockport County fans ..."

At about the same time, one of the intrepid band of County supporters, Stuart Hart, was leaving Oakwell in dismay. I must now digress slightly to state that I have always enjoyed the way in which James Alexander Gordon reads the football results. You can tell whether it is a home or an away win from the way in which the names of the teams are emphasised:

Clydebank 0, STIRLING ALBION 2

MOTHERWELL 3, Hibernian 1

Or, if the match is a draw:

carlisle united 1, rochdale 1

– with the name of the away side being delivered in an almost sing-song tone to denote the equality of the score.

And so, shortly after 5pm, the depressed Gerry McEvoy was negotiating the bends on the A6 between Disley and High Lane (even the kids were quiet) and the disgruntled Stuart Hart was approaching Woodhead, when James Alexander Gordon duly stated:

"Barnsley 4, Stockport County 4."

The look of shock on McEvoy's face was replaced by one of sheer alarm as he narrowly avoided colliding with the 199 bus.

"No, they must have got the score wrong." I said.

"Definitely 4-4," said Gerry, "No doubt about it. You can tell by the tone of voice when it's a draw."

I fumbled desperately with the radio, trying to get Radio Manchester for confirmation of what we had just heard. Simultaneously, the mixed emotions running through the mind of Stuart Hart resulted in his just avoiding an argument with the signpost for Penistone.

I bought a "Football Pink" about an hour later but the report, sent in to meet a tight deadline, contained only the details of the pasting that County had been receiving. However, there was quite an interesting addendum at the foot of the front page:

LATE SCORER: BRADD (Stockport) 83, 86, 88.

I have often wondered how many County fans came within inches of

Les Bradd

losing their No Claims Bonus at about five past five on that February afternoon.

Gigg Lane

Like most away grounds visited with some frequency, I have mixed feelings about this place. My most vivid memories are of April 1981 and December 1996.

In April 1981, Les Bradd, whose amazing feat just over two years earlier had nearly caused highway carnage, was not on hand to repeat the effort. He, like manager Jimmy McGuigan and several other players had been stranded by the freak late April snowstorms, living as they did in the Buxton, Chesterfield and Sheffield areas. John Henshaw, David Booth and myself were our representatives at this match with Gerry McEvoy having been "grounded" on kids' party duty. We were almost wishing that we had met with the same fate, as the Albatross, late in setting off as usual, was overtaking everything in sight round by the Worsley interchange. To make matters worse, the local radio informed us at that stage that County only had seven players available. We were incredulous. Surely the game would be called off? County, staring re-election in the face, would be heavily fined and maybe even kicked out of the league.

As we neared Bury, the man on the radio told us that two more County players had turned up and that the game would go ahead. We entered Gigg Lane in trepidation, certain that we were about to witness the biggest hiding in County's none too illustrious history. For some reason we had bought stand tickets and arrived at our seats just in time to see twenty players take the field.

Fact 1: County were such a badly run outfit at that time that star player, Terry Park, had been given the day off to get married!

Fact 2: The previous Tuesday, promotion chasing Bury had walloped Scunthorpe United 6-1.

Fact 3: Stockport born Craig Madden was scoring almost at will and would finish the season with 42 goals to his credit. It would be another 15 years before County were to implement a decent youth policy. Ironically, Madden would play a major role in that enterprise.

Fortunately, the law forbidding goalkeepers to pick up back passes had not yet been set up and David Lawson duly did so, straight from the kick off. This was accompanied by hoots of derision from the Bury fans. According to Jim Iley, the Bury manager, if the referee had kept due note of Lawson's time wasting, the match would have finished about midnight! Not only did Lawson waste as much time as he could, he also made some excellent saves as the nine men bravely kept Bury at bay. Half-time arrived with the match still goalless and we could sense that both the players and the supporters of Bury were becoming increasingly frustrated.

Out came the teams for the second half and ... surprise, surprise! ... County now had eleven men! Dave Sunley and Chris Galvin had managed to battle through the snow from Sheffield. The match, however, continued to be somewhat one-sided. Neville Southall in the Bury goal remained a frozen spectator and the score remained 0-0. A point would give County a fighting chance of avoiding re-election. With about ten minutes remaining, Dave Booth said: "You know, we haven't had a single shot at goal yet. When we do, I bet we score."

Before I had the chance to tell him not to be so daft, Martin Fowler duly made County's only attempt at goal, his 20 yard effort zipping into the net beyond the reach of the frozen Southall.

A few dodgy moments as Bury laid siege to the County goal and that was it – victory snatched from the very jaws of disaster. Jim Iley's face was an absolute picture. I don't think he could comprehend what had happened. He wasn't the only one.

Over the years, I have been to Gigg Lane on several occasions, but the match in December 1996 – the Saturday before Christmas in the season when Bury and County ended up as Champions and Runners-up respectively – sticks in my mind because I can't remember ever feeling so cold at a football match either before or since.

Only four of us had decided to brave the cold. Paul Thompson, son of David, myself and my son Craig, had decided to meet at David Booth's house and then, sensibly it would seem, travel to Bury in one vehicle. When Craig and I pulled up outside the Booth residence, we immediately spotted Paul but there was no sign of either resident, Dave or his partner, Jackie, who, it turned out, had gone shopping. Soon, however, we saw the familiar Austin Maestro turn into the road from the A6. David was a painter and decorator and had been delayed finishing off a job.

"Have we got time for a cup of tea?" he asked in a tone of voice which implied that he was going to have one anyway. While we were having a drink, we debated as to whose car would make the journey to Bury.

"We always go to home games in yours." David said to me, "So it's only fair that we go in mine."

"As long as it's got a decent heater," I replied, mindful of the cold air outside and the fact that the temperature appeared to be dropping to a Siberian level at a fairly steady rate, "and a radio so that we can listen to the results on the way home."

"Course it has," he said, looking at me gone out.

We duly removed all the paint tins and bottles of white spirit from the back seat of the Maestro and set off for Bury a little bit later than originally intended. As the weak December sun started to set over Whitefield at about 2.30pm, I noticed that the temperature in the car had grown decidedly chilly.

"I thought you said that this car had a good heater." I remarked.

"It does," replied the driver, "but it isn't working at the moment."

"You can't argue with logic like that." I thought, my feet like blocks of ice as we walked towards the away fans' entrance.

The match was a hard fought but fairly unremarkable 0-0 draw, and a satisfactory point gained for County. The only incident on the pitch that I can recall with any clarity occurred just before half-time. Paul and myself, having been nominated to go and fetch some hot drinks were passing just behind the Bury goal. Bury keeper, Dean Kiely and Brett Angell went for a 50-50 ball. There was no doubting either the commitment or the courage of either player and the outcome was a juddering collision which left both players laid out on the frozen pitch. It was with relief that we saw both of them back on their feet shortly afterwards, apparently none the worse for wear.

Happy with this end to the first half, Paul and I continued in our quest for the hot drinks that our hypothermic bodies were craving. I will always remember our return journey to our seats. Both of us were shivering so much that a scalding mixture of coffee and Bovril kept spilling over our trembling hands. As we left the ground, I was not looking forward to our trip back to Stockport in Booth's mobile fridge. We hadn't had the radio on as we travelled to Bury since we had spent much of the time discussing the situation at the top of Division 2. It was no surprise to find that the radio like the heater, failed to function.

The Shay

I have already mentioned the 1-0 defeat there in 1969 and have no desire to recollect further details of it. However, a trip to this ground in May 1990 proved to be one of the most dramatic afternoons imaginable.

"I bet it will be chaos getting into the ground," I said to whoever was listening, "Remember what it's been like at County when a team chasing promotion has brought a lot of fans." A year earlier, the kick off at Edgeley Park had been delayed whilst thousands of Rotherham fans were attempting to get through one turnstile. Rotherham, as expected, clinched promotion with a 3-1 victory over a fairly inept County side cobbled together by recently arrived manager, Danny Bergara.

However, in 1990, the boot had been placed quite remarkably on the other foot. If I remember correctly, County needed to win at Halifax and, if Peterborough managed to beat promotion rivals Southend, then County would be in the third automatic promotion place. A whole gang of us descended on Halifax – not just the "old lags" but most of our offspring plus pals as well. As expected, the scene both outside and inside the stadium was chaotic.

I can't remember the exact sequence of events but we ended up being split up into several smaller groups and I was with my son, Craig and his pal, Tim Hesketh. Craig and Tim were only eleven at that time and had no chance of seeing over the thronged mass of County fans in front of us, some of whom were already spilling over the barriers on to the running/ speedway track that surrounded the pitch. It was then that we noticed Dave Booth who had made his way almost to the front. We managed to join up with him but it was obvious by now that the two boys were not going to be able to see much in the packed enclosure. It was then that Booth came into his element. Grinning all over his face, as was his wont, he proceeded to persuade a rather attractive WPC that it would be a good idea to let County fans accompanied by children into the half-empty family stand occupied by Halifax fans. We were allowed to pass behind the goal, Dave having adopted Tim as his son for the afternoon. As we were being escorted by this rather splendid policewoman, we noticed Dave Thompson in a fairly central position of the crowd.

"Have you been arrested?" he shouted.

"No, but I wish I had," replied Booth, grinning lecherously at our escort.

Not only was this young lady very attractive and pleasant, she was also a very sensible police officer. Several other groups of "lads and dads" joined us in the family enclosure. We were welcomed by the Halifax fans and a good atmosphere prevailed all afternoon. Halifax had peaked in the early 1970s but had been in decline ever since. It was no surprise, therefore, that there was a certain amount of empathy between both sets of fans. The match did not begin very well for County with Neil Matthews playing superbly for Halifax and putting them 1-0 up half way through the first half. However, whatever Danny Bergara had said during the interval, whether it was something to do with laying the foundations of a bungalow or not, it certainly seemed to do the trick. County began to play more positively and Matthews started to fade out of the game. (His next goal in the football league would be for County). A blatant penalty was denied us by the referee before Chris Beaumont raced through to equalise. With about fifteen minutes remaining, Ian McInerney scored what proved to be the winner and sent County fans into a state of delirium.

As the minutes ticked away, with Halifax fighting back and laying siege to the County goal, the news filtered through to us that Peterborough were winning 2-0. This information went all round the County fans and the noise became deafening as we roared them on. The score must also have been communicated to Danny and the players, as their jubilation at the final whistle seemed to indicate that promotion had been achieved. When both players and fans learned that Peterborough had, in fact, lost 2-0, the realisation was devastating. Many Halifax fans in that family stand were genuinely upset for us. (I was so pleased to see them win the Conference and do well in their first season back in league football).

When we finally got back to where our fleet of cars was parked, there was more bad news for one of the members of our squad. Lawson Shield is a Geordie who has lived in "exile" in Stockport for over thirty years now. Although a County season ticket holder, Lawson is still a big Newcastle fan. Needless to say, he was not best pleased to learn that Newcastle had emulated County's feat and failed to gain automatic promotion on the final Saturday of the season.

Given the circumstances of the match at Halifax, County's double demise at the hands of Chesterfield was no real surprise, even though they had beaten the Derbyshire side quite comfortably (3-1) at Edgeley Park some three weeks before. And poor old Lawson – Newcastle fared nearly as badly as County losing quite comprehensively to Middlesborough!

Saltergate

I went to Chesterfield twice in the 1989-90 season. The first occasion was to watch an entertaining 1-1 draw back in November. The second visit was to witness the 4-0 drubbing which followed the false euphoria of Halifax.

Unfortunately, I missed the most dramatic County match at that ground through having to work. Of course, Brett Angell's fifth minute winner, Tony Dinning's goal line clearance and the marvellous saves of Paul Jones have all been well-documented. My personal memories of the occasion are as follows:

* I left work in Macclesfield at about ten past nine.
* I switched on the car radio, pre-tuned to GMR.
* I learned that County were leading 1-0 and under some pressure.
* I was certain that Chris Beaumont would score for Chesterfield.
* I reached Poynton. John Jeffers joined Paul Rooney in the commentary box. The 90 minutes were up.
* I reached the lights at the "Five Ways". "How much more time can the ref add on?" moaned both Rooney and Jeffers.
* I turned right at the lights and parked up in front of the off licence unable to drive any further.
* The rain was absolutely torrential.
* If there had been any passers-by on such a wretched night, they would have seen a deranged lunatic sitting in a parked Fiat Panda, tearing out what little of his hair remained and shouting "Get the —— blown, you stupid ———!"
* "I'm out of here," said Jeffers, "I can't stand this any longer."
* I thought of doing the same thing myself and returning to the car a few minutes later, but I remember Stuart Hart telling me once that he always regretted walking through deserted streets for about forty minutes on a certain July afternoon in 1966. I wondered if he was wandering about at that moment somewhere in Chesterfield.
* I stayed put. The rain drummed down on the roof of the car. I had another go at the referee. This time he did as he was told. County were in the top half of the football league for the first time in over 60 years!

Prenton Park

I must admit to not having been there for a number of years. My fondest memory is of a trip there in November 1965 to watch a first round cup-tie. We went in Dave Thompson's Austin A40 (anybody remember them?), and the brakes were sticking. Not content with subjecting ourselves to a ride of terror, we had to witness a nail biting finale as County clung on desperately to a fluke 1-0 lead given them when a half-hit shot from Johnny Price brushed the legs of Tranmere defender Eddie Stuart and changed direction just enough to deceive the goalkeeper. Stuart, of course, joined County the following season and became a key figure in the 1966-67 Championship winning team.

Haigh Avenue

I was eleven years old when I saw my first match at this ground. It was August or September 1956. Trevor Porteous played the first of his 364 games for County and we won 1-0. That was the last match County ever won at Southport.

The reward for the somewhat fortuitous victory at Prenton Park in 1965 was a second round trip to Southport. The result was an exciting 3-3 draw, after County had led 2-0 and Southport 3-2. An effortlessly struck penalty from David Shawcross earned County a replay which they contrived to lose 2-0.

I also went there in 1970 to watch a 1-0 defeat. Hughie Ryden was denied an equaliser by the hard pitch. Poor Hughie did everything right, heading the ball down towards the corner of the net in a style of which Jack Connor would have probably approved. Unfortunately, the ball landed on a bump, reared alarmingly and bounced over the bar.

Belle Vue

The first time that I visited Belle Vue was in the 1965-66 season. All that I can recall about this match, apart from the fact that we lost 1-0, was the referee having to stop the match to warn two County players – Frank Beaumont and Norman Sykes – because they were about to thump each other!

I saw a memorable game there at the start of the 1972-73 season. A mad dash across the Pennines on a Friday evening had been occasioned by a very good start to the season, County having embarked upon the League Cup run which was to bring them victories over two

First Division sides. Our efforts seemed to have been worthwhile as, with just a couple of minutes remaining, County were holding on comfortably to the 1-0 lead
given them by Paul Hart. Then disaster struck. County crumbled and Doncaster scored twice in a minute. The Doncaster players and fans were still celebrating and we were getting ready for a miserable journey home when I gave a cursory glance in the general direction of the pitch just in time to see Eddie Garbett race through a static Doncaster defence to equalise with practically the last kick of the match.

Vale Park

I have made surprisingly few visits to Vale Park, given its geographical proximity. The last time was in the early 1980s to witness a 4-1 beating administered to County on one of the few occasions between 1970 and 1990 that they managed to reach the second round of the FA Cup.

I can remember a match there in the 1965-66 season. It resulted in a 2-0 defeat. The thing that I remember most about this match, or rather the only thing that I remember, is Frank Beaumont "pinching" about thirty yards as he waited to take a throw-in while an injured player was receiving treatment. This was accompanied by great mirth from the County fans and much disgust from the Vale fans. The referee was supervising the treatment of the injured player, but the linesman had nothing else to do but fail to notice Beaumont's antics and endure the wrath of the Vale fans. It is perhaps as well that County were unable to take full advantage of the attacking position that Beaumont had engineered for them.

Meadow Lane

I went to a lot of away matches in 1965-66. The means of transport this time was Stuart Hart's Hillman Husky van, a splendid vehicle which gave sterling service in support of the cause. This was the only time I have ever been to Meadow Lane or, indeed to a football match in Nottingham, having been put off by Forest's over the top prices in 1997-98. County won the match 2-1 but once more the mists of time have erased all but one incident from my memory. All I can say is that the turnstile attendant at Meadow Lane must have been as dopey as the linesman at Vale Park, having watched two friends, bearded

Arnie Gleave and his wife, Lesley, six months pregnant, enter the ground through the turnstile marked "JUNIORS"

Millmoor

Not a bad ground, as far as luck goes. However, it always seemed to be a filthy, gloomy day and the journey back over the Woodhead Pass in the November, December or January dark was never a pleasant one. However, the return journey was made bearable in 1972-73 after a second round FA Cup victory, and a rare highlight of the following season, a 2-1 victory when Harry Kirk gave one of those virtuoso displays that he used to keep in special reserve.

Bloomfield Road

It so happened that County were due to play their first league match of 1981-82 at Blackpool. For some reason, the big kick off was later than usual and this match took place on the Saturday before the August Bank Holiday Monday. Someone had decided that we should make a family weekend of it, taking wives and children with us and stopping over on the Saturday night. The idea was that the men folk would attend the match while the women and children would spend Saturday afternoon amid the beer cans and dog turds on Blackpool beach. Believe me – I do not exaggerate, although much has been done to clean it up since that era.

It cost a fortune that night on Blackpool Pleasure Beach, the hotel was grotty and County lost 2-0. Bloomfield Road itself would probably be described by the Estate Agency of the Blackpool Chairman as being "ideal for the Do-It-Yourself enthusiast".

The match itself was quite remarkable for two reasons. Firstly, County started off playing superbly. Blackpool fans behind us in the stands were saying that they looked a better team than Manchester United who had played there in a Testimonial match a few days earlier. Needless to say, County were unable to maintain this standard for the second half of the match or, indeed, for the rest of the season. The other noteworthy feature of the game was that Tommy Sword missed a penalty! I am pretty sure that this was the only one he missed throughout his entire career with County. When this happened, County were already losing 2-0, having missed a hatful of chances in the first half.

The Racecourse Ground

I have only been there once and that was once too often. It had started off as a lovely spring day and I went with my son to watch the last match of the 1985-86 season. By 3pm, the weather had turned foul. Trevor Matthewson was sent off for retaliation after being the victim of a high tackle and a nasty gash. County surrendered meekly, lost 3-0 and the spectre of 1986-87 was looming inexorably.

Anfield

Nearly twenty years after their "finest hour", County returned to Anfield, this time in what had by then become the Milk Cup, I think. Whatever drink it was sponsored by, the competition again provided County with the opportunity to contrive another glorious exit. They had done extremely well to hold Liverpool to a goalless draw at Edgeley but a sound beating looked to be on the cards at Anfield. Manager Eric Webster (it would have been interesting to see what he might have achieved if he had had a bit of money to spend) had cobbled together a fairly makeshift side from County's injury-hit squad. Mike Salmon had what was probably his best ever game in goal for County (earning much praise from the sporting Bruce Grobelaar), as the Fourth Division "no hopers" withstood wave after wave of Liverpool attacks. Sadly, Paul Bowles received a career-terminating injury (County's luck hit an all-time low in this respect in the 1984-85 season), but the rearranged side were holding out as the last few minutes of normal time ticked away. Suddenly, Dean Emerson chased a ball booted hopefully out of defence and found himself in a race for a 50-50 ball with Grobelaar. Were we about to see the sensation of the season? As the two players collided, Emerson prodded the ball past the Liverpool keeper and watched in anguish like the rest of us as it rolled just wide of the post. Extra time was too much for the heroes who had run themselves into the ground. Michael Robinson and Jan Molby scored for Liverpool and County departed to a standing ovation from both sets of supporters.

Gresty Road

I have already mentioned the dreadful performance which brought on such a feeling of foreboding in 1976. However, another visit which comes to mind was a strange match in 1970 which County, who were doing quite well in Matt Woods' first full season as manager, won 3-2.

The third goal was one of the strangest I have ever seen. The ball skidded across the edge of the Crewe penalty area to Bobby Elgin who, totally off balance stuck out a foot in the general direction of the ball to send it flying into the top corner of the net as he fell flat on his back. County also scored another "goal", a cross-shot from Johnny Price actually caused the net to bulge just inside the post. Team mates were busy congratulating Price as a Crewe defender scooped the ball out of the goal and booted it up the field. The referee was the only person in the ground who had failed to see the ball go in the net and was at a loss to understand why the players had stopped.

I also went to Gresty Road for the first match of the 1996-97 season. It was a boiling hot day. Only Tim Hesketh and myself bothered to go. Everyone else was either working or on holiday. County lost 1-0, the winner coming about four minutes from time. Our verdict – not very optimistic. I wasn't very impressed with the new goalkeeper, Jones, who looked a bit shaky at times and didn't seem to have a very good understanding with the defenders in front of him. Alun Armstrong looked to be out of touch and the midfield combination of Marsden and Bennett would have to do a lot better.

Maine Road

They did do a lot better, of course, and what a shame that Jones, Armstrong and Marsden were no longer County players when the Hatters returned to Maine Road after an absence of nearly forty years. Tom Bennett was also absent from the County ranks, having suffered that awful injury at Birmingham. Hopefully, he is by now back to full fitness and able to resume his role as a key player for County. This afternoon was not a pleasant experience because, as well as having to watch County lose 4-1 in what was a pretty poor performance, I was also forced to witness the degrading spectacle of County fans fighting amongst themselves in front of me. The best thing about the match was when young Aron Wilbraham scored County's equaliser. Surely, this must be a "first" in the history of football – a season ticket holder scoring a league goal against the team he supports! With County's reserve games played in mid-week, had he not been promoted to the first team, Aron may have been sat in his usual spot supporting City! As my friend and former colleague, City fanatic Ian Armstrong was moved to point out: "That could only happen to City!"

Spotland

Yes. The pies are fantastic! Which is more than can be said about most of the football I've watched there. My last visit there was in September 1990. Rochdale had made a very good start and were top of the league at the time. Danny Bergara returned to visit his former employers with a team which played Rochdale off the park. Result? Rochdale 1 County 0.

Boundary Park

No matter what time of year you go to this ground, it is always freezing. The only time I saw County win there was my first ever visit in 1956. The result was 4-2 and I can remember Alan "Digger" Daley miscuing a centre and slicing the ball straight into the Oldham net.

14

When Friday Night Was County Night – Part 3

It was in the middle of the 1960s when County began to play most of their home matches on a Friday night. Basically, this was a good idea. If you played football yourself on a Saturday afternoon, it meant that you had the chance of watching your local team a lot more. However, the real reason for the switch to Friday night was the close proximity of the big Manchester clubs.

Some thirty-five years ago, a match at Old Trafford was accessible to the average local fan and, apart from travelling expenses, would cost a United fan who lived in Stockport only slightly more than a Fourth Division game. There were also quite a lot of people living in Stockport who, first and foremost, supported either City or United but who had a soft spot for the local club. This meant that, by playing their matches on a Friday night, County had the opportunity to attract the "floating" fans.

The "Friday Night is County Night" era was enhanced by the championship season of 1966-67 and the two subsequent decent seasons in the Third Division. However, for the 1969-70 season, the rules were changed by the Football League in that the gate money was no longer shared between the two clubs, but rather kept by the home team. This, of course, meant that the club which was doing well would keep all the extra revenue from their increased support. Clubs like County could no longer look forward to a decent pay day to compensate for the beating they would get when playing the league leaders away from home.

This rule change meant that other clubs, especially if they were situated some distance from Stockport, were no longer pleased to come to play at Edgeley Park on Friday night. What did it matter to them now if they played before 2500 or 2000 fans? Another factor was the money from the football pools. You had to be on the coupon for x number of matches in order to qualify for the full pay-out.

It transpired, therefore, that most of the home matches played in County's worst ever season took place on a Saturday afternoon. The standard of play ensured that gates would have been very low no matter when the matches were played.

In the early seventies, impassioned pleas from the directors of Tranmere Rovers and County, based on obvious geographical factors persuaded the Football League authorities to listen to reason and Friday night football returned once more to Edgeley and Prenton.

But what did this mean to the average supporter of such a team? Fundamentally, it meant that you got home from work as quickly as possible through the rush-hour traffic, bolted down something to eat, said a fond farewell to your family and vanished into the chilly November or the freezing December/January night to go and join some 2000 other lunatics in a crumbling stadium for the doubtful pleasure of watching your favourite football team fail to beat what was usually pretty mediocre opposition.

As throughout the seventies and eighties, County staggered from one crisis to another, and attendances dropped below 2000 with alarming frequency. Getting to Edgeley Park on a Friday night became practically an obsession. If you didn't turn up for home matches at least, you felt that you were letting them down. For me, a satisfactory season was when I had attended the vast majority of home matches, seen four or five away games, and experienced the sheer pleasure of my team having finished the campaign outside the bottom four.

I am very proud of the fact that, on 6 May 1985, I was one of the elite 1480 who saw County stuffed 3-0 by Halifax Town as, from a position of comfortable mediocrity in March,

Played 31, Won 11, Drawn 7, Lost 13, Points 40,

– they had managed to plunge relentlessly towards the depths of despair to finish with a record of

Played 46, Won 13, Drawn 8, Lost 25, Points 47.

But why this obsession with getting to the ground for the Friday night match when you knew that the likely outcome was to be similar to the events of 6 May 1985? This affliction was suffered by some 1500-2000 other poor souls. At home, I must have burbled on about County to some extent without realising it. One day, round about 1977, I entered my living room to find my daughter, Sian, then aged three, kneeling opposite the sofa in the process of arranging an assortment of soft toys in a line thereupon.

"Now you sit there, Mansfield. And Tranmere, you can go there."

As she placed a battered looking Womble called "Rochdale" in the middle of the sofa, the awful realisation dawned on me that I was responsible for my daughter naming all her soft toys after Fourth Division football teams.

"Wouldn't it be better to call the Womble 'Wimbledon'," I suggested.

The frown and the knowing look that I received told me that I had better not argue my case. (out of the knowing looks of babes and infants ...)

It is a little known fact that when HM the Queen walked out on to the hallowed turf of Edgeley in the year of her jubilee, it was the first and only time that a monarch has entered the stadium of a football league club. There is absolutely no truth in the rumour that the Royal Family won 2-0.

And so, into the eighties, and things were not getting any better. The micro-chip was starting to revolutionise life as we knew it but, apart from the odd lick of paint now and again, Edgeley Park and all who sailed in her continued to deteriorate slowly but inexorably. During that dire autumn of 1986, as disaster followed disaster, I took some consolation from the computer game of "Football Manager", which I had begun to play addictedly on the computer bought for my children the previous Christmas. If you played it at Level 1, the obstacles to your producing a successful team were appreciably fewer. On the Friday night following the FA Cup defeat at Caernarfon, I masterminded our rise from the bottom of the Fourth Division, through a record-breaking League and Cup double and took County all the way to the final of the European Cup. I didn't realise how adept I had become until the screen flashed up the final score:

AC MILAN 1, STOCKPORT COUNTY 9

The following day, County managed to beat Cardiff City 2-0 and I decided it was time I grew up.

15

Heroes in Adversity

No-one could argue that 1969 through to 1989 were the worst years in County's history. The fact that the club kept going for long enough to interest Brendan Ellwood and pave the way for the exciting Ellwood – Bergara era is in itself a miracle.

The club was probably kept afloat by the bargain basement sales of players such as Freddie Goodwin, Johnny Price, Paul Hart and later, Mike Salmon, Dean Emerson and Mick Quinn. They all went for ridiculously cheap prices in order to keep the taxman, bank manager or bailiffs away. Even now, when County's credit appears to be much better, the tendency to sell the best players seems to be continuing.

Fortunately, there has always been someone, or a body of people, who have been on hand to keep the club going. In the 1960s, the names of Bernard, Porteous and Quigley spring to mind as the ones who worked a bit of magic when it was needed most. In the 1970s, Lukic (he didn't really need Stockport County) and Kirk, with the latter digging deep into his financial reserves right up until his death. If my memory serves me well, it was action from directors Dave Hunt and Graham White which paved the way for the entrance of Brendan Ellwood. Whatever may have been said either for or against all these men, I think that it would be very unfair to suggest that any of them did not have the best interests of the club at heart.

As County finished off the 1970s with a 3-1 defeat at Wigan, we were of the opinion that, surely, the next decade could not be any worse. We were right. It was just as bad. As the "Iron Lady" trashed picket lines and the Argentine junta with equal force and disdain, we were told that the lady was not for turning. (I've never been sure what that phrase meant, but then I've led a fairly sheltered life). The message to the likes of Stockport County, though, was fairly clear. Unless they could manage to pay their way, smaller football league clubs were not for saving.

Throughout the decade, football was plagued by disasters which, when you look at footage of games in the 1970s, played on a paddy-field in front of thousands of standing, unsegregated fans, were disasters just waiting to happen. The knock on effect of the catastrophes which occurred in Brussels and Bradford meant that smaller clubs were obliged to modernise their grounds with money that they didn't have. To be fair to the "Iron Lady", however, it has to be said that funds were made available in this respect from the Football Trust.

As County waved farewell to the 1970s in a similar fashion to which they had begun the decade, with a resounding defeat, who would have thought that, within the next ten or eleven years, the Cold War would be over, the Berlin Wall reduced to rubble, Apartheid ended, and County promoted to Division 3?

The government-inspired ideology that every organisation had to be cost-effective found its way into the boardroom at Edgeley Park. In order to economise, the staff had to be as small as possible. Fifteen, or sixteen, if we were lucky, was about the number of players from which the managers of that era were able to choose. This meant that there was little competition for places. You had to play really badly to be dropped. More significantly, willing work-horses were often required to play when they were not fully fit. I am fairly certain that several players had their careers shortened by this practice.

Let's go back and see how things stood at the start of the 1980s. !979-80 was one of the better seasons round about that time as County managed to finish in a lofty sixteenth place. This was achieved by dint of winning the last match of the season for the first time for seven years. Eddie Prudham scored a hat-trick in the 4-1 win over Halifax and was given a free transfer for his pains.

I have gone on at length about the victory at Bury in the 44th match of the following season (1980-81). This was followed by another win, this time at home. Goals by John Rutter and Terry Park saw off Mansfield Town and ensured that re-election was avoided again (just). The customary defeat on the final day (2-0 at Hereford) was academic (just).

However, the highlight of this season had occurred way back in September when County had achieved a notable "first", becoming the first team from Division 4 ever to beat a Division 1 team in a two-legged cup tie. They held Sunderland who, at the time were riding high having won 4-0 at Maine Road the previous weekend, to a 1-1 draw at Edgeley Park. County's goal was scored by David Sunley

John Rutter scores County's first goal against Mansfield Town on 1st May 1981

who stooped to head home a raking cross from Tony Coyle at the Cheadle End. I was in the main (only) stand for this match and, below me, in the paddock, a small section of Sunderland fans were subjecting Oshor Williams to a shameful tirade of racial abuse. They were quite taken aback when he turned round and told them what he thought of them in his Geordie accent.

The second leg at Roker Park proved to be County's biggest celebration for years. It was too far for me with work the next day, so I can only rely on the reports of the time, some of which I have kept, not just because it was a glory night for County, but also because of the sheer naffness of the headlines. Apparently, County had been playing very well but trailed 1-0 with just twenty minutes remaining. The commentary match on the local radio was interrupted and, expecting to hear "more bad news for Stockport County fans", I was astounded to learn that Sunley had equalised. Back to Maine Road or Old Trafford or wherever the commentary was coming from. Then, a few minutes later – "We are going over to Roker Park where a penalty has been awarded." I thought, "Well, that's our lot for another year." But – "Sunley was brought down when clean through." said the commenta-

Dave Sunley powers in a header against Sunderland

tor.. Up stepped Tommy (May his mangelwurzels always be free of ragwort) to provoke some crass headlines in the following day's papers.

SUNDERLAND PUT TO THE SWORD

SWORD CUTS DOWN ROKER MEN

SUNDERLAND SLASHED BY SHARP SWORD

Unfortunately for Sunley, his name does not lend itself so easily to such newspaper wit and he was, therefore, denied his fair share of the glory.

Headlines like those helped to raise Tommy Sword to the status of a cult figure at Edgeley Park and such reverence was no less than he deserved. While still on the subject of silly headlines, the best Tommy Sword one that I saw came after he capped a superb all-round display with the only goal of the match against Sheffield United the following season.

SHARPNESS OF SWORD BLUNTS BLADES was, I think, down to the "Daily Mirror".

I can't lay this topic to rest without stepping forward in time to 1996

"And, at last, some good news for County fans." Tommy Sword scores the winner from the penalty spot against Sunderland.

and awarding the gold star to the "Stockport Express". After Luis Cavaco's magnificent solo effort at Upton Park, had earned County a replay and Ian Dowie the chance to become an Edgeley Park legend, the "Express" came up with the gem: CAVA-COCA COLA.

It took a little while for the penny to drop before I realised that "Cava" is the equivalent of champagne in Portugal.

I must not digress any further. Back to the eighties and the serious business of survival ...

1981-82, which had begun so brightly, for half an hour or so at least, in the Blackpool sunshine, was to follow the same pattern as the two previous seasons, although without the same level of desperation that accompanied our visit to Gigg Lane. Being 18th, at that time, was not too bad, and there were one or two matches that stood out. There was a very entertaining 4-2 victory over Aldershot, with Tony Coyle scoring twice in what was one of his best games for County, and the 1-0 defeat of Sheffield United which prompted the execrable headline regarding Tommy Sword. Perhaps the highlight (and the lowlight) of the season involved goalkeeper, Brian Lloyd. After leaving County for Southend, Wrexham and Welsh international honours, Brian had returned to County via Chester, replacing David Lawson at

County, 1980-81

the start of that season. A reliable goalkeeper, he only missed one match in the two seasons of his second spell at the club. One game he probably wished he had missed took place on a blustery night at Valley Parade. With the wind at his back in the first half, Lloyd's clearance went sailing up into the air and down into the Bradford net to put County 1-0 up. Unfortunately, playing against the wind, neither Lloyd nor any of his colleagues could repeat the feat and Brian went on to concede five second half goals to more than compensate for his "pièce de resistance".

He must have wondered whether becoming one of the select band of goalies to score a goal from open play had brought him bad luck as, in the next match at home to Rochdale, he conceded another four as County produced one of those Friday night performances guaranteed to produce acute indigestion in their supporters who had eaten too quickly in order to get to the match on time.

It was shortly after this defeat that County changed their kit, forsaking the light blue Argentina type stripes because of the conflict in the Falklands. Tumbledown wasn't just in the South Atlantic either, as County managed to win just three of their last eighteen matches.

1982-83 and a semi-respectable 16th position. Thinks: "20th, 18th,

16th – if we continue to progress at this rate, we should end up second in 1990-91." – Russell Grant, eat your heart out.

In the close season, Eric Webster had pulled off a masterstroke, namely the signing of Mick Quinn from Wigan on a free transfer. At first he looked overweight (he was) and unlikely to score many goals. However, after watching Quinn make his debut in the first match of the season when County were unable to hold on to a 1-0 lead against a Peterborough side weakened by two sendings off, I spotted Jack Connor on the way out and asked him his opinion of County's new centre-forward. To my surprise, the man who had worn that number nine shirt with such distinction some thirty years earlier gave Quinn his seal of approval, with the added comment, "He needs to lose some weight and learn not to retaliate right under the nose of the referee."

Mick accepted the first piece of advice but I am not all that convinced that he accepted the second. It was while Quinn was suspended for clobbering somebody that the exotically named Michael Wardrobe took his chance to score twice in the 3-2 win over Tranmere, prompting such wit from the terraces as,

"This lad will become part of the furniture at Edgeley."

However, this was not to be and indeed, in the next match, the entire team played like fitted wardrobes in the 7-0 mauling that they (not to mention the handful of travelling fans) suffered at the hands of Hull City. In fairness, the lads showed a lot of grit and bounced back the following week with a 3-2 win at Northampton. One of the goals was scored by Mike Power, a young part-timer who was starting to look a very good player. This made me feel a bit old. I used to play for the same team as his dad!

Mick Quinn returned from his suspension and took his total for the season to twenty-four, the last of these coming in a 3-0 victory over Colchester United which meant that County had fifty-four points and that re-election had been avoided as early as 22 April! The usual poor finish was not avoided, though. No goals and three defeats, one of these inflicted by promotion bound Port Vale, whose number ten, a certain Ernie Moss, had an infuriating habit of scoring against County. How I detested the man!

Moss duly kept up the sequence, scoring Vale's second and nearly provoking a riot as both sets of fans celebrated. Vale fans for obvious reasons, County fans because Alan Kirk had once again dipped into his pockets – this time to settle a debt to the Inland Revenue and ensure that league football would be seen again at Edgeley Park the following August.

1983-84 ... and 12th. County finish a season in the top half of the league table! Fantastic! Well, not really, when you consider the team that Eric Webster had put together on a shoestring budget. Before financial necessity meant that Mick Quinn was sold to then Second Division Oldham Athletic, with Joe Royle getting an absolute bargain at £52,000, County's first choice eleven was usually:

1. Salmon, 2. Rutter, 3. Sherlock, 4. Emerson, 5. Sword, 6. Thorpe, 7. Williams, 8. Evans, 9. Quinn, 10. Jones, 11. Coyle.

Not a bad player in the team. Three went on to play in the top flight. Six played over 250 games for County, with Andy Thorpe and John Rutter playing a great deal more. Clive Evans would have emulated the others, had Colin Murphy not persuaded him to join Lincoln City. Graham Jones only spent the one season at County but looked to be quite a decent player.

It was quite a good season, then. The only moments of despair were the 3-0 FA Cup debacle at the hands of Telford United and a Friday night indigestion inducing 4-0 home defeat dealt out by Mansfield Town. Some three weeks later, County tried out the public relations exercise of allowing kids in free if they were accompanied by an adult. This meant that four of us got into the main stand for the price of one adult ticket. The experiment was made even more worthwhile by the fact that County managed to put four past debutant Peterborough goalkeeper, David Seaman, two each for Tony Coyle and the recently arrived Steve Taylor. Other spectators were perhaps not too impressed by having the main stand full of kids. It was most embarrassing when, at half time, one of my young companions knocked a cup of orange juice over the two guys sat in front of us. As they got up to survey the state of their clothing, I recognised one of them as former United star Willie Morgan and the other as a member of the singing group "The Batchelors" who had been quite successful in the 1960s. Willie Morgan was quite amused by the whole affair but his companion was not best pleased to see his rather expensive coat covered in orange juice. For one dreadful moment I thought he was going to exact a murderous revenge by singing "I Believe" to us. However, he soon calmed down and refused my offer to pay for his coat to be cleaned. County's customary end of season malaise set in after this match and they contrived to lose three of their last four games, the only win coming at Hartlepool where a thronging mass of 790 spectators saw the home team go down 2-1.

Having finished in such an exalted position, we could look forward with some hope to 1984-85. Mick Quinn had departed, of course, but we had two seemingly decent strikers in John Kerr and Steve Taylor who had both arrived in the second half of the previous season. We were also able to rely upon the players who had become the backbone of the side, namely Salmon, Rutter, Sherlock, Emerson, Sword, Thorpe, Williams, Evans and Coyle. Indeed, the season began very well with a 4-1 win over Hartlepool. That afternoon, England's cricketers were batting in a Test Match against Sri Lanka. I got back to the car and found out that County had scored more goals than they had runs!

Prior to the second leg at Liverpool, County were doing well:

Played 10. Won 4. Drawn 2 Lost 2. Points 14.

Perhaps it was the effort of taking the champions to extra time or the fact that injuries were taking their toll earlier than usual but four successive defeats sent County plunging down towards the bottom of the league. The slide was halted by a fine 3-1 home win over Port Vale who had been relegated (again) and were chasing promotion (again). County's form remained inconsistent, however, and they were unable to get out of the bottom half of the table. It looked as if a lower mid-table position would be achieved at least, after two successive home victories (6-0 v Aldershot and an excellent performance to beat league leaders Swindon Town 2-1 on 1March). When County managed to beat Colchester United 1-0 three days later, their record was:

Played 28. Won 10. Drawn 6. Lost 12. Points 36.

As safety can be loosely described as fifty points, County had another eighteen games in which to cobble together another fourteen points. No problem? With County nothing is straightforward. Oshor Williams had been transferred to Port Vale, Andy Thorpe was a long-term casualty and Steve Taylor and John Kerr had left the club bound I know not where. With the transfer deadline fast approaching, County had about twelve professionals on their books. With no money available to add anyone to the squad, several of the players we relied on had to play when obviously not fully fit. The inevitable happened:

Played 18. Won 3. Drawn 2. Lost 13. Points 11.

The magic target of fifty points was not reached and the spectre of re-election would once again spoil the early summer for County fans. A 2-0 win at Exeter on 20 April was the last flicker of sunshine in County's spring of discontent, although they were then still some way above the re-election quartet. Unfortunately, the best result they could manage from the remaining games was a 0-0 draw at Rochdale.

But why this dismal run-in? Only 1480 of us saw the last home match, a particularly putrid performance as Halifax Town won 3-0. I would say that too few people had been asked to do too much – the players who remained and the manager, Eric Webster who was to pay the inevitable price for what, surely given the circumstances of this season, could not be considered any shortcoming on his part.

As Darlington administered the "coup de grace", thereby gaining promotion for themselves, County's plight and the disappointment of re-election were put into perspective by the tragedy that was unfolding at Valley Parade.

The legislation which followed the disaster at Bradford meant that it was mid-September before County were able to play a league match at Edgeley Park. The new manager, Colin Murphy had, ironically, been present at Valley Parade, when his Lincoln City side were the visitors on that dreadful day.

County managed to overcome this disadvantage quite well, winning three and losing two of the five away matches in question. However, as they were not receiving any money in gate receipts, the financial situation was dire and the £12,000 needed to secure the signature of Paul Smith (5 goals in 7 games during his loan spell) from Sheffield United, was not forthcoming.

My son, Craig, had already been to County a few times before and I took his pal, Tim Hesketh, with us to watch the second home match of the season, a 2-2 draw against Chester City. Fifteen years have passed and Tim is still an incorrigible County fanatic, having become a victim of the addiction referred to in the first paragraph of this book.

Smith looked to be a very good player, scoring both County,s goals in a match in which an unknown player signed from Newport County, Trevor Matthewson, made his debut. Not long afterwards, Colin Murphy left rather abruptly to go and work in Saudi Arabia. Les Chapman became player-manager and, in my opinion, did a fairly good job. Murphy's departure didn't seem to have too adverse an effect upon the fortunes of the team and a good level of consistency was achieved. The daftest thing that occurred that season, apart from the inexplicable sacking of Chapman at the end of it, involved winger David Mossman who had played quite impressively since being signed by Murphy early in the season. Now, a well-known star player could not get away with this, although Mossman did for a short while. When booked at Port Vale, he told the referee that his name was Paul Smith. This was a bit silly since the latter's name wasn't even on the team sheet as he had returned to Sheffield United when County couldn't afford to sign him.

This incident occurred during a great run of form between late October and Christmas when County won seven and drew two of the nine matches played. To put the record straight regarding Mossman, he played no small part in this effort, scoring four of the eighteen goals that County notched up in this period. Mark Leonard was scoring regularly and becoming a firm favourite with the fans. Even with the odd slump in form, County were still in with a good chance of finishing in the top four at the end of March. When two goals from Leonard and a Tommy Sword penalty gave County a 3-2 victory at Scunthorpe on 31 March, things were looking quite promising:

Played 38. Won 18. Drawn 11. Lost 9. Points 65

But then –

Played 8. Won 0. Drawn 2. Lost 6. Points 2.

The dreaded end of season disease had struck again as this abysmal run culminated in the dire display at Wrexham referred to previously.

It was farewell to the last of those players who had worked so hard to keep County going through the first part of the decade. John Rutter had played his last game for County and so too had Andy Thorpe, for the time being. Tommy Sword and Tony Coyle departed to Hartlepool and Chesterfield respectively. Mike Salmon had been transferred to Bolton for £18,000. Amongst all the P45s flying around at the time there was one for the manager also. Was it all Les Chapman's fault that County had such a poor end to the season after doing so well for so long? According to the board, it must have been.

During the close season, Jimmy Melia was appointed manager and we were informed via the local press that Edgeley Park was "buzzing with optimism".

16

The Great Escape

"And Smith must score" is the title of the Brighton fanzine. With the bitter humour of the condemned, it refers to the incident when Gordon Smith, having burst through the Manchester United defence found himself with the goal at his mercy and, with the score at 2-2, had the chance to perpetrate the biggest Cup Final upset of all time. Unfortunately for Smith, manager Jimmy Melia and all Brighton fans, this was not to be. Brighton lost the replay 4-0 and Jimmy Melia was to end up a few years later as manager of Stockport County.

No matter how hard I try I cannot remember some of the players who represented County in the autumn of 1986.

The season began with a 3-0 defeat at Swansea – disappointing but not enough to set the alarm bells ringing just yet. This season was, of course, the first one when there would be automatic relegation to the Conference. The defeat at Swansea was followed by a 2-1 victory over Tranmere in the League Cup. This result provoked a bit of optimism but we didn't realise how bad Tranmere were, especially when they returned three days later to win 2-0 in the league.

Things started to look a bit bleak when, in the next match, County received a 4-0 thrashing from Exeter and lost Paul Hendrie with a broken leg. The only crumb of comfort, if such it can be deemed, was when the "Football Pink" printed the league tables upside down to show Stockport County sitting proudly at the top!

In the second leg of the League Cup, County drew 3-3 at Tranmere to set up a second round tie with Sheffield Wednesday. In the league, County maintained their level of consistency, losing regularly both before, after and during their epic encounters with the Yorkshire side.

During the sixties, I had lived in Sheffield for four years and, in about a dozen visits as a neutral to Hillsborough, I had never seen Wednesday win. I was out of the country when they won 5-3 in a League Cup match at Edgeley round about 1968. Therefore, the first time I saw Wednesday win a match was on a grisly November day back in 1976 and there are no prizes for guessing who there opponents were! Then in the Third Division, they were drawn at home in the first round of the FA Cup. Standing behind the goal, Dave Booth and myself had a good view of Rodger Wylde scoring for Wednesday and Ian Holbrook missing the ball completely and punching John Rutter in the head! To put the lid on a splendid afternoon's entertainment, I got out of Dave's car outside my house and stood right in a pile of dog crap, not realising I had done so until I was half way down the hall. Just what you need after a 2-0 defeat.

Anyway, back to 1986 and the next meeting between the two teams. In the context of performances so far, I suppose that a 3-0 defeat at the hands of a First Division side was not too bad a result. Furthermore, it seemed to be the lifeline that manager Melia needed to clutch at as he proclaimed enthusiastically that his team would give everything in the second leg. His enthusiasm must have communicated itself to the board of directors because the match was diverted to Maine Road, in order to accommodate the hordes of fans who would be desperate to watch it. As it turned out, the 2089 of us that turned up constituted probably the lowest ever attendance at a first class match at Maine Road, with the rain soaked County contingent dumped in the away fans' enclosure.

The weather on that October night was as wretched as County's performance. Missing the injured Paul Hendrie and Bill Williams, County had a dearth of decent players. Trevor Matthewson was magnificent and he was supported manfully by Clive Evans, Levi Edwards and Andy Hodkinson. On-loan goalkeeper, Simon Farnworth made several good saves but had to pick the ball out of the net seven times as the difference in class between the two teams was painfully obvious. It was an embarrassment for Wednesday to have to play us. Add to this the circumstances under which we were forced to watch this massacre and the fact that it was preceded by a 5-0 hammering at Cambridge three days earlier, and it is not difficult to understand why the few remaining County fans were not happy fans.

10 October 1986 – the best Saturday of the season so far! We didn't have a match! When play resumed, the torture continued. Mark Leonard, whose goals had got County so near to a promotion place the previous season had been transferred to Bradford City. Disappointment at losing one of our better players was tempered by the notion that, had he stayed at County, he would have failed to achieve much playing week after week in such a rotten team.

And so the dire autumn continued. Whenever I hear Barry Manilow warbling that awful ballad about October, I think that a fitting punishment for inflicting such torture upon the unsuspecting radio listener would have been forcing him to watch a County match in October 1986. However, they did manage to get one point during that dreadful month, Wayne Entwistle scoring in a 1-1 draw at home to Colchester – the highlight of the season up to that point. This was after Oshor Williams, now with Preston North End, had returned to haunt his old pals, playing magnificently in his team's 3-1 win.

Jimmy Melia's last match in charge was the 3-1 defeat at Aldershot on 9 November. In a period of five weeks there had been eight league matches. County's record was:

Played 8. Won 0. Drawn 1. Lost 7. Points 1. For 4 Against 20.

By then County were so far adrift at the bottom of the league that we were wondering if Edgeley Park would be deemed fit enough to stage Conference football. Throw in the 10-0 aggregate League Cup walloping and it is a wonder that 1338 of us were still daft enough to go and watch the 2-1 home defeat by Hereford on 3 November.

I can't remember what happened, or what we were told happened, behind the scenes at Edgeley Park round about that date. Suffice to say that there was a lot of disagreement in the boardroom. Dragan Lukic was ousted, Jimmy Melia sacked and Colin Murphy, having returned from the desert, became County manager for the second time.

Whatever happened behind closed doors – we were given to understand that Dave Hunt and Graham White played major roles – it was certainly for the good of the club. If action had not been taken then, I am sure that there would be no Stockport County Football Club in existence today.

And so Jimmy Melia left for pastures new. He seemed a decent enough bloke but he could not have inflicted more mass torture if he had been a designer of sackcloth Y-fronts for the Spanish Inquisition.

Murphy returned just in time to preside over another of County's most ignominious hours. If the second leg of the Sheffield Wednesday fiasco was the nadir of watching County, then the first round FA Cup defeat by Caernarfon Town was the absolute pits. It must rank as one of the darkest days in the history of the club. From a personal viewpoint, the only good thing about it was that I didn't go. Newspaper reports told of hooligan County fans going on the rampage in the centre of the town. All I can say is that I don't know where they all came from. At the home match a fortnight earlier, there weren't enough fans for a decent argument.

The following week when County played host to Cardiff City, Welsh pride was restored as Cardiff fans duffed up Castle Street. County pride was also restored as, with the right kind of fighting spirit instilled in them, they beat Cardiff 2-0. I have already mentioned the euphoria caused by Levi Edwards' goal. The Christmas lights brightened up the town centre and County had won their first home game of the season.

Colin Murphy now began to rebuild the team around the reliable players at his disposal. His first signing was Les Robinson, a young player who was unable to command a first team place at Mansfield. Robinson is living proof that Murphy had an eye for a bargain where decent players were concerned going on to spend several seasons with Oxford United where he was the team captain.

Although the next match was a 1-0 defeat at Hartlepool, there were signs that things might be getting a bit better. County then fought out a 0-0 draw at Southend with on loan keeper, Andy Gorton, making a good start to his County career. This was followed by a 2-1 home win over Wrexham, Clive Evans and Vernon Allatt scoring in what was County's best performance of the season so far. We were now able to look forward to the Christmas fixtures with a bit less trepidation, especially when we learned that Murphy had signed Ernie Moss and Phil Brown from Chesterfield on Christmas Eve.

Boxing Day saw another 0-0 away draw, this time at Lincoln who were then lying sixth. The next day, a Vernon Allatt hat-trick disposed of Peterborough (3-1). This meant that County had avoided defeat during December. The run continued in the new year with a 2-1 home win over Crewe, a1-1 draw at Cardiff and a 0-0 draw at home to Exeter. Much criticism has been levelled at Colin Murphy and his long ball tactics. It certainly wasn't pretty but it was no longer pathetic. In Ernie Moss, Murphy had acquired an ideal target man who was able to either hold the ball or lay it off accurately to a colleague.

Having been eliminated from all cup competitions, County only played the three league matches in January. When they lined up at Molyneux on 7 Februaury, they had not lost a league match since 28 November!

Not surprisingly, County went down 3-1 at Wolverhampton. The mood of optimism continued, however. Gates began to edge above the 2000 mark again as people became aware that perhaps the lost cause was not entirely lost. Successive victories over Halifax (2-0) at home and Scunthorpe (2-1) away were followed by two disappointing home draws (0-0) v Torquay and (2-2) v Orient. The Orient match was particularly disappointing as County had lead 2-0 with goals from Allatt and Robinson with only minutes remaining. Nevertheless, the run of form since the beginning of December meant that we were off the bottom, having won five and drawn six of the last twelve matches.

Just when you think it's safe and what happens? A disastrous run of four consecutive defeats is what happens. County were once more the league's 92nd club and in with a very good chance of being the first one to be relegated automatically to the Conference. It was during this period that Vernon Allatt lost favour with the manager, probably because he contrived to miss quite a few chances in the 1-0 home defeat by Burnley. In any event, he never made County's starting line-up again. This was a pity because he had played a useful part in the team's revival.

County needed desperately to beat Cambridge on Friday 27 March, a day which dawned full of ill-omen. An evil north westerly lashed the country, bringing with it squally showers and structural damage. As the day wore on and the rain became torrential and incessant, I was wondering whether the match would go ahead. County had signed goalkeeper Chris Marples, another arrival from Chesterfield, as Andy Gorton's loan period had expired. What a night for a goalkeeper to make his debut! We also welcomed back Tommy Sword, on loan from Hartlepool.

The floodlight pylons were trembling in the wind and there was enough flickering to suggest that there could be a power cut at any time. Debris from a nearby builder's yard had been blown on to the Cheadle End terracing. The storm-lashed Railway End was devoid of Cambridge fans.

As County kicked off against a Force 9 gale, it soon became apparent that Nature's dynamism was not the only element we had to battle against. In order to save this person embarrassment and myself having to hire a solicitor, I shall not reveal the identity of METHANE MAN. This person had spent most of the afternoon in the pub as a work-mate of his was leaving to take up another job. We were to learn during the course of the evening that he had consumed six pints of bitter and three curried black puddings. It was not long before he became the nearest County fan to the Railway End with 1620 hardy souls standing upwind of him. As Methane Man was busy creating his own private gale, the three ex-Chesterfield players began to do County proud, with Brown and Moss skilfully keeping possession of the ball and Marples defying Cambridge and the elements. Marples must have been wondering what he had done to be making his debut on such a vile night as shots came in at him from all angles. As the referee blew his whistle for half time, a handful of rain drenched Cambridge fans appeared on the Railway End. Held up by the dreadful conditions, they had missed their team's two goals. On the Pop side we were quite optimistic about County's chances since the storm force wind was showing no signs of abating.

An early goal was needed and Tommy Sword duly obliged from the penalty spot after Phil Brown had been tripped. The crowd, sensing that we could go on and win, really got behind the team as the appalling conditions added to the entertainment.

In one incident, Keith Branagan in the Cambridge goal raced out of his area to kick clear and then turned in startled anguish as the gale blew the ball back over his head for a corner. A massive roar (yes, from only 1600 or so fans, or was it the wind?) greeted Phil Brown's equaliser, and when Andy Hodkinson scored what proved to be the winner, we all went slightly mad. Unfortunately for me, the back-slapping celebrations contrived to place me downwind of Methane Man who had still not finished having his say in the proceedings. Even the ensuing lung-searing blast of noxious gas could not diminish my euphoria. It was easy enough now to defend a lead with a gale at their backs and County duly won the match 3-2, a victory which proved to be very significant. If County had lost that match, confidence would have been at a very low ebb after five consecutive defeats and I don't think that they would have avoided the drop.

Skilfully avoiding giving a certain person a lift, I went home, retrieved my TV aerial from half way down next door's garden, slurped a four pack of Boddington's and went to bed happy.

A fairly desperate 0-0 draw with Aldershot was in store for us the following Friday. The only good things to come out of that match were a badly needed point and the promise extracted from one of our number that he would never eat curried black puddings before a County match again.

The next three matches were all victories and went a long way towards ensuring County's safety. A 3-0 win at Prenton Park with goals from Ernie Moss and Andy Hodkinson (2) pushed Tranmere deeper into trouble. This was followed with a 2-1 win at Hereford and a 1-0 home win over Scunthorpe when Ernie Moss scored the goal of the season.

Not even a 5-0 drubbing at Crewe on Good Friday, when a certain David Platt helped himself to a hat-trick, could set the alarm bells ringing too loudly, and County returned to winning ways on the Easter Monday with a 1-0 victory over Lincoln City who had started to slide down the table at quite an alarming rate.

A 0-0 draw at Wrexham the following Saturday and a 3-1 home win over Swansea meant that County were more or less safe. Incredibly, after such a dreadful start, they had now accumulated the magic fifty points. This meant that the usual abysmal end to the season could be accommodated without too much worry. County, needless to say, duly obliged with a draw and three defeats.

On 8 May, the crowd that attended the 2-0 home defeat at the hands of Southend numbered nearly 3000, and most of us came away quite happy. A few months before we could have been forgiven for thinking that this would be the last game of league football ever staged at Edgeley Park. Nobody moaned too much about the result, knowing how hard the players had fought to preserve the league status of the club. Those who had arrived during the course of the season (Robinson, Moss, Brown and Marples) had all proved to be valuable acquisitions. Trevor Matthewson (who played in every game but one), Bill Williams, Levi Edwards, Andy Hodkinson, Clive Evans and Wayne Entwhistle had battled away throughout the dramatic nine months.

County's rise to the dizzy heights of nineteenth meant that Burnley, Torquay, Tranmere and Lincoln were involved in a nerve-racking last day of the season. The match against Southend had been staged on the Friday night but, had County still been in danger, it would have been moved to the Saturday. It was the first time ever that matches from the bottom end of Division 4 were featured on national radio. The fact that it was Lincoln who succumbed was to have, ironically, fairly serious repercussions on the set up at Edgeley Park.

17

The Friendly Football Club

At the time of his departure, many County fans thought that Asa Hartford had been unfairly treated and I must admit that I was one of them. Although I wasn't very impressed with the actual style of play, there was a distinct improvement, results-wise, over the previous season – Hartford's first and only season in charge.

He had inherited a bit of a shambles, Lincoln City having deprived us of Colin Murphy and Murphy in turn having deprived us of several of our better players. However, it was nothing like the mess that Murphy himself had walked into some ten months earlier. Things didn't go too badly at first but County spent most of the season struggling in the bottom five. It was only because the other dysfunctional County, Newport, who not long before had been playing in the European Cup Winners' Cup, were so badly adrift that there were hardly any worries at all about dropping out of the league.

During the course of the season, the manager made some quite popular signings. Bob Colville from Oldham looked a very useful player and soon became a firm favourite with the fans. However, Hartford.s most popular acquisition was Frank Worthington who had been sacked from his job as player-manager at Tranmere. Although pushing forty, Worthington was still a class act. Indeed, if Ernie Moss had still been at the club, County would have had a striking partnership with a combined age of just under eighty! In one home match, someone remarked that Worthington had been booked the previous week for retaliation, having thrown his bus pass at the opposing centre-half.

Apart from the pleasure of being able to watch some of the fantastic skills that still remained in Frank Worthington's repertoire, the season was notable for one or two other items. For the first time in years, County actually made it through to the third round of the FA Cup. What is even more remarkable is that they were able to beat two non-league sides en route – Telford United after a replay, when Chris Marples saved a first minute penalty (revenge at last!), and Runcorn away. This set up a third round tie at home to Frank Clark's Leyton Orient. County managed to lose 2-1 after taking the lead through Colville just before half time. My lingering memory of this match is the courage of one of Orient's defenders who put himself in the path of an absolute pile driver from Steve Bullock and knocked himself unconscious in the process. As his side celebrated their passage to the fourth round, little did their manager realise that some ten years later he would be leaving Edgeley Park in a much more subdued frame of mind!

Another good signing made by Hartford was the return of Andy Thorpe on a free transfer from Tranmere. Thorpe was to play another 200 or so games for County and, fittingly, to captain the club to promotion in 1991. I still find it hard to forgive Thorpe for what he was to do to me some two years after his return. In Danny Bergara's first full season in charge, County's form had become somewhat erratic and they had started to fall down the table. On a freezing day in early February, County were trailing 1-0 against an Aldershot team who were not far from the bottom of the league. County had thrown players forward in an attempt to snatch an equaliser. With everyone but Dave Redfern in the opponents' half of the pitch, the ball was played down the left leaving an Aldershot forward with a clear run on goal. Thorpe, quick to spot the danger, raced across the pitch and booted the ball into touch with all the force he could muster. It smacked right into the side of my head! The temperature was slightly above freezing and there was a cold February wind. It is not hard to imagine therefore, the discomfort that I felt. I noticed that Dave Booth's hands were in close proximity to my face.

"What are you doing?" I asked irritably.

"Just warming my hands on your ear."

Anyway, back to 1987-88. The downside was that the tactics seemed to consist of players running around like headless chickens and, with the notable exception of Frank Worthington, blasting the ball in the general direction of the other team's goal at a velocity comparable to that of the Andy Thorpe effort which nearly knocked me into Sykes's reservoir.

To cause further aggravation in a not very entertaining season, the team's disciplinary record was appalling, with the manager himself at the forefront of the yellow card queue. One masterpiece of skulduggery in the home leg of the Tranmere league cup tie left an opponent rolling in agony and provoked their goalkeeper, one Eric Nixon, to race forty yards from his goal to try and exact some sort of revenge. Fortunately for all concerned, Nixon was restrained by some of his team mates. In fairness to County's player manager, it has to be said that he had been a superb player for most of his career. Frustration at his own dwindling pace and the lack of skill of some of his players was the likely cause of the petulance that he was wont to display on numerous occasions.

County were safe for about the last third of the season and once again had the leeway which enabled them not to win any of their last five matches. Wayne Entwhistle took it upon himself to outdo his manager by getting himself sent off in the last two meaningless games. I can't remember who else was sent off in the last match at Scarborough, but County's nine men held out for a 1-1 draw.

Asa Hartford now had the close season to try and put together the basis of a decent team and he wasted no time. He acquired the services of Rodger Wylde, who was still County's best striker when he took a too early retirement, Mark Payne from Dutch side Cambuur, Brian Butler from Blackpool and Andy Gorton from Oldham to replace Chris Marples who had been transferred to York City. Judging by Gorton's displays when on loan to County, it seemed that he would be a more than adequate replacement. Tony Coyle returned to County from Chesterfield just before the start of the season and another newcomer was Nigel Hart, brother of Paul.

County began well with a 4-1 win at Darlington but it wasn't long before a strange pattern began to emerge. Throughout the entire season, County failed to win two consecutive matches and it was not until the last two games that they lost two in succession. In total they drew 21 matches, won just 10 and lost 15.

About half way through the season, County signed a local lad called Tony Hancock who immediately began to make an impression. Hancock was undoubtedly a player of some talent but the subsequent managerial upheaval may be one reason why he failed to live up to his early promise. In the end, though, he was transferred to Burnley for quite a sizeable fee.

This was also the time that County were trying to build up an image of being a "family club" and the phrase "The Friendly Football Club" was coined. On entering via the Cheadle End to make my way to the Pop Side around Christmas time, I was surprised to be greeted by

Brendan Ellwood who handed me a mince pie. The product hardly compared with the home-made variety but at least it was a gesture. Somehow, I can't imagine Martin Edwards emulating this action at Old Trafford. I have the feeling that he might be told where he could stick his mince pies in any case.

There was nothing friendly about the reception afforded to Colin Murphy when he returned to Edgeley Park with his promoted Lincoln side just before Christmas. After Bill Williams had scored what proved to be the winner from the penalty spot, the chants of "Murphy, Murphy, what's the score?" were decidedly lacking in seasonal spirit.

Other matches which spring to mind in the early part of 1989 are: the 4-0 defeat of Exeter in which Tony Hancock came on as substitute to devastating effect; a 3-0 victory over a very mediocre Rochdale side; and a 0-0 draw with soon to be doomed Darlington, whose goalkeeper, Nigel Batch, performed heroics to earn his side what, at that time, was a very valuable point.

These last two matches were to prove to be quite significant. When Asa Hartford was sacked for no apparent reason other than the fact that County were going nowhere fast, many people thought that the dismissal was unjust. There had been a definite improvement over the previous season when the departure of Colin Murphy and several key players had caused a lot of disruption.

Even more surprising was the appointment of his successor. Danny Bergara's Rochdale had looked to be a far worse team than County. Moreover, Hartford had brought in a fair bit of useful cash via the transfer market by selling the likes of Les Robinson to Doncaster Rovers and Chris Marples to York City. (Yes, they were much better equipped clubs than County in those days). He had also managed to find adequate replacements who cost nothing. Only the signing of Brett Angell for £32,000 (then the club record) seemed to be a waste of money. He had also done the amazing lease-lend, buy back at half the price deal which involved Manchester City and Bill Williams.

And so, the word on the street was that the new manager would be well-advised to go back to Rochdale, or better still to Rocha. This sentiment became even more apparent as County's by now notorious end of season "malaise" began to establish itself a little earlier than usual. They failed to win any of their last twelve matches, although they did manage to draw eight of them. The new manager constantly changed the forward formations. Colville, Caldwell, Wylde, Hancock and

Angell were "chopped" by Danny Bergara far more than by opposing defenders.

Andy Gorton was shown the door and Nigel Batch arrived on loan from Darlington. Somewhat erratic, but very agile, this guy was hugely entertaining. It was woe betide any unsuspecting opponent who found himself with a clear run at goal and only Batch to beat. The new keeper's technique was to race as far as possible out of the penalty area, commit GBH on the unfortunate opponent and then protest to the referee that it was a complete accident. He wouldn't get away with it today, of course, but I can remember the feeling of anticipation, waiting for the sickening thud as County's fairly square back line was breached. In the last game of the season, with thousands of Rotherham fans packing the Railway End to cheer their team to promotion, this tactic nearly led to a riot when Batch brought an abrupt end to one of their attacks by booting both forward and ball into the Hardcastle Road paddock.

I believe that Danny tried to sign the "Wild Man" but the deal fell through. Batch returned to Darlington where the following season he was to achieve something, which, I believe, is unique in the history of football. Having been a member of Colin Murphy's Lincoln side which resurrected itself after one season in the Conference, Batch emulated the feat with Darlington, thus becoming the only player ever to help a club to regain its lost league status on two occasions.

18

"We Had Joy, We Had Fun, We Had Seasons In The Sun ..."

1989-90

In the summer of 1989, the recently appointed Danny Bergara had been extremely busy. Many players had left and there was a host of replacements. From Bergara's former club had come Malcolm Brown, Chris Beaumont and David Frain. Brown became an immediate favourite with the fans but injury denied both Beaumont and Frain the opportunity to establish themselves until later in the season. George Oghani had arrived from Burnley and the new manager had signed two goalkeepers – Barry Siddall from one of his umpteen clubs and David Redfern from Gainsborough Trinity. Ian McInerney came on a free transfer from Huddersfield and the manager paid out the princely sum of £3000 to Sheffield United for Darren Knowles.

The £50,000 paid to Rochdale for David Frain was the club's record transfer fee and this was soon to be beaten by the £60,000 paid to Hull City in order to obtain the services of Keith Edwards. In the previous season, Edwards had scored thirty times for Hull who were then in the second division. Although he had now reached the veteran stage, Edwards was still a top class striker and it was a great shame that he and Danny Bergara were to fall out later in the season.

County began with a 1-1 draw at home to Torquay and then secured their first win under Danny Bergara by beating Third Division Bury 1-0 in the League Cup. They followed this with a 0-0 draw at Burnley and a 1-1 draw at Bury in the second leg. This was followed by yet another draw – 2-2 at home to York when Chris Marples was given a tremendous ovation by the home fans. Into September and Mark Payne provided me with a very welcome birthday present, securing the first league victory of the season by scoring the only goal of the match at Wrexham. David Logan repeated this feat at Maidstone and County found themselves in the top half of the league for the first time for ages. The following Friday saw Brett Angell score as many goals in one match (4) as he had managed throughout the previous season. His manager said that, although Angell had scored four times, he hadn't given him the impression that he would score many more. Whether this was a psychological ploy or a linguistic error, I am not sure, but Angell's response was to score six times in the next five matches.

County's winning run was halted by a 2-1 defeat at Aldershot. I can't remember them ever winning there. Henshaw once took it upon himself to travel down to Hampshire and was rewarded for his pains with the privilege of being able to witness a 7-0 thrashing. At this point, enter Keith Edwards. Bergara and Edwards went back a long way to when they were both at Sheffield United and the striker with more than 250 league goals to his credit made public his regard for the Uruguayan's coaching ability. The addition of Edwards had a beneficial effect upon the already improving Angell who was now starting to make the £32,000 look like a bargain basement sale. It took Edwards about ten minutes to score his first goal for County, unhurriedly "passing" the ball into the net through a crowded penalty area, in the 3-2 defeat of Scarborough. This match was followed by three more victories with Angell and Edwards scoring for fun and suddenly County were top of the league.

Not only were they getting the results, they were scoring plenty of goals and the football was a pleasure to watch. The master craftsman and his fast learning apprentice were a strike force to be feared. Full backs Brown and Logan were prominent both in attack and defence, Bill Williams and Andy Thorpe were strong in the middle of the defence and, in midfield, County could rely on the skills of Mick Matthews, Mark Payne, Ian McInerney and John Cooke.

In the second round of the League Cup, County gave First Division QPR quite a scare in the first leg at Loftus Road despite trailing 2-0 after about ten minutes. This match gave rise to a dreadful joke that went the rounds at the time – "I thought County had won 3-2. It said on the radio that Ian, Mac and Ernie had scored."

The cup-tied Edwards was inelegible for this tie and County could have certainly used his services in the second leg when a fine performance by David Seaman ensured that the match ended 0-0.

In the league, County's progress was halted by a 2-0 defeat at Peterborough, which allowed Exeter City to take over at the top. In their previous home game a 1-0 victory over Southend had deposed the Essex side from the top spot. They now had the chance to do the same thing to Exeter. This proved to be easier said than done. McInerney gave County the lead and Angell missed a penalty before Edwards made it 2-0. Then Exeter pulled one back and reduced our nerves to a frazzle as they laid siege to County's goal for much of the second half. Player-coach, Paul Jones, deputising in Andy Thorpe's normal role, as the latter had been drafted into midfield to cover for the injured Mark Payne, stopped a shot on the line in the dying seconds of the match. The ball spun up in the air and Jones had to perform a remarkable juggling act to keep it out.

Even with one or two slumps in form, County remained well in contention until February and March when things started to go a little bit haywire. Easter Saturday was the time when County's luck ran out completely. The visitors that day were the eventual champions, Grimsby Town. County had to play practically the entire match with ten men after Paul Jones had been sent off in the very first minute. They trailed 2-0 and then 3-1 and things looked even bleaker when Bill Williams sustained a fractured jaw. Bravely, he attempted to play on but was made to retire by his manager who later came out with one of his linguistic masterpieces:

"You could see his guts all over his face."

Then McInerney made it 3-2 to set up a thrilling finale, Grimsby scoring with practically the last kick of the match.

So that was that, it seemed. A disappointing end to a season that had begun with such promise. The Easter Monday trip to Spotland looked as though it was just going to be a token gesture. This was definitely the case as County trailed 1-0 for most of the match. We were just about to leave the ground as about two minutes of injury time had already been played, when David Frain took it upon himself to equalise with what was, literally, the last kick of the match. County grasped this lifeline avidly and proceeded to win their next three matches in fine style. Firstly, they beat Carlisle 3-1 at home with the recently arrived Jim Gannon scoring his first goal for County. This was followed by a fine 2-0 victory at the Abbey Stadium. (Cambridge had been having a great run and were to become the eventual play-off victors). Next, another 3-1 win, this time over promotion rivals Chesterfield in front of over 5000 fans , set up the dramatic afternoon at Halifax and the anti-climax of the play-offs.

If the journey home from Halifax seemed to take ages, it was nothing compared with the Sunday afternoon procession through the Peak District National Park after the 4-0 defeat at Chesterfield.

1990-91

I would say that Danny Bergara'smost noteworthy attributes were his ability to re-motivate players after failure in the play-offs and his capacity for signing unheard of players and converting them into very effective members of the team – this aspect being particularly pertinent to those who played in the forward positions.

Brett Angell, twice the player he was at the start of the 1989-90 season, had been the division's leading scorer with 28 goals. Promoted Southend had managed to prize him away from Edgeley Park and, courtesy of the tribunal's decision, County had received their first ever six figure transfer fee. They would receive another nice windfall a few years later when Brett went to Everton.

Paul Cooper replaced the departed Barry Siddall as first-choice goalkeeper, with the manager unwilling to place his full trust in the eccentric Dave Redfern who, although signed essentially as cover, would play a major role as the season reached its dramatic climax. Three unknowns had also arrived from the north east, a couple of young players from Hartlepool Reserves, Tony Barrass and Lee Todd, and a forward or central defender, also from Hartlepool, called Paul Williams. County already had a Paul Williams, signed a year earlier, who had decided to wait until this season before making an impact – probably just to confuse everybody.

Strangely enough, because of injuries and other reasons known only to the management, and the subsequent transfer of Paul A Williams (ex Hartlepool), the two Pauls and Bill Williams only played together in one match, although County were represented by two of the three Williamses on many occasions. Confused? I most certainly am.

The major purchase in the close season was Neil Matthews who had played so impressively against County the previous May. However, injuries and lack of fitness would mean that he would have to wait until the following spring before grabbing centre stage.

Ironically, the first match of the season was at the Shay and the attendance was less than half the number that had witnessed the dramatic encounter of a few months before. Not much drama unfolded this time, however, as the two sides treated us to a boring 0-0 draw.

The first home game of the season was against Burnley in the League Cup and this didn't bode very well either, as the visitors cruised to a 2-0 victory.

"One decent season and that's it. Same as usual, bottom of the league or not far off." That was the general opinion as we left the ground after that match.

On the following Saturday, just over 2600 turned up to watch the first home league match of the season against Walsall. You could sense that a victory was desperately needed to boost the confidence of the team. It was apparent straight away that the players were trying very hard, perhaps too hard because things weren't going very well at first. However, once Chris Beaumont had given County the lead, they began to play in a more relaxed manner and showed themselves to be clearly the better side. Mark Payne added a second and, to his obvious and immense delight, Paul A Williams bagged a third.

Some interesting and even exciting matches followed. County lost 1-0 at Rochdale after dominating almost the entire game. They drew 2-2 at home to Burnley, a real "blood and thunder" encounter, in which two goals from Mark Payne rescued County who had been trailing 2-0.

In the mid-week game County beat Carlisle 3-1 before travelling to Cardiff on the Saturday. Unable, or more likely unwilling, to travel all that way to watch the match, I decided to spend most of that afternoon battling against the weeds that were threatening to turn my back garden into something resembling the set of "Day of the Triffids". At about 3.15 I came in for some much-needed refreshment and tuned in to GMR. I can remember the exact dialogue between the studio linkman and the commentator at the match.

"Over to Ninian Park to see if there has been any improvement in the condition of Stockport County."

"I'm afraid there hasn't. In fact, it's become even worse. Cardiff went three up after twelve minutes when..."

Off went the radio and back on went the gardening boots.

This time it wasn't James Alexander Gordon who provided the sensation of shock mingled with delight. Having decided that it would be kind and eco-friendly of me to leave the rear of my house to the flora and fauna of the neighbourhood, I went inside and switched on the TV. A quick flick on to Ceefax and I found that County's condition had improved considerably. Neil Matthews had opened County's account and a late effort from Chris Beaumont had further reduced the deficit. And then the tell-tale flicker on the screen. Up went the name "Williams" and County's score changed to three.

"YEEEES!" I shouted, and the cat shot in startled fright from the windowsill where it had been asleep behind the curtain.

Apparently, the introduction of substitute, Keith Alexander, had made all the difference in the second half. Alexander, who had just been signed from Grimsby, was to have a short and fairly unhappy stay at Edgeley Park. The fact that Paul A Williams had injured himself when scoring the equaliser meant that the new arrival was due for a nine game run in the first team – a run that would prove to be fruitless from the point of view of goals scored. I felt really sorry for him in what proved to be his last game for County. Lincoln City were being beaten 4-0 when Alexander lashed the ball through a crowded goalmouth into the roof of the net. His long awaited celebrations were curtailed when the referee disallowed the goal for an infringement.

With Paul A Williams restored to fitness, Alexander was left out for the next match, at home to Darlington who had climbed back out of the Conference and now were the league leaders. Played on a filthy afternoon in early December, this was a superb match with Williams, Gannon and Payne scoring in the 3-1 win. Not only were we going to Edgeley Park expecting County to win these days, but we also expected them to score freely. Progress was such throughout November and December that, when Paul R Williams entered the scene to score twice at Scarborough a week or so before Christmas, the 2-0 win put County top of the table.

They were to contest this position with Darlington and Hartlepool for the rest of the season. With five teams due to be promoted from the Fourth Division in order to sort out the numbers for the Premier League set up, we sensed that County's best chance was now. Just to keep their fans in a state of anxiety, County entered 1991 slightly off form.

Any sporting events were put into perspective by the anti-humanitarian and ecological horrors that were being transmitted nightly into our living rooms from the Gulf War. From the comfort of our firesides we were able to witness the damage that could be done by SCUDS, SAMS and other devilish devices designed to obliterate anything or anybody unfortunate enough to get in the way of them. However, life goes on regardless and Danny Bergara pulled off a master stroke which led as much as anything to County's eventual success. He signed a player capable of unleashing a different type of missile. Apparently, he had read in the "Football Pink" that Andy Kilner had returned from playing in Sweden and was looking for a club in the north west. And so, for the price of a "Football Pink", County signed a player who was to have a tremendous influence on the rest of the season.

Before Kilner and since, County have had players capable of delivering a long throw-in (Trevor Porteous and Mike Flynn spring immediately to mind) but not with the force, accuracy and flat trajectory of Kilner's efforts. To this, add the fact that he was a speedy winger with a fierce shot and the ability to send over a decent centre or two and you have a recipe for success – for a while at least! Kilner marked his full debut with the two goals that defeated Wrexham and immediately became a favourite with the fans. This match was followed by three more wins on the trot and things had started to look pretty good once more. Unfortunately, three successive defeats followed, two of which could have proved to be particularly costly – 3-2 defeats at the hands of promotion rivals Hartlepool and Burnley.

The manager came up with a possible solution to the team's lack of form, by signing two strikers, Jason Lee from Charlton Athletic and Kevin Francis from Derby County. Both played in the 3-0 win at Lincoln, Paul A Williams being ruled out through injury again. I didn't go to Lincoln but the report said that Francis, having come on as substitute, had made Beaumont's second and County's third goal with a superb run down the wing and cross into the area. When I saw the edited highlights on TV, I felt obliged to disagree. It was more of a lope than a run, with his massive strides enabling him to leave defenders trailing in the wake of his size thirteen boots. As he neared the penalty area, he appeared to lose control of the ball, slid and lunged at it and managed to knock it into the path of the oncoming Beaumont.

The following Tuesday, County were at home to Cardiff and, with Williams still unfit, the new striking combination was unveiled to the Edgeley faithful. Jason Lee looked to be quite a good player and County were looking to extend his loan period into a permanent stay. On the other hand, I was surprised to learn that County had paid something in the region of £40,000 for Francis. As the match progressed the general consensus of opinion around where I was standing was that we had acquired a bigger, clumsier version of Keith

Alexander. Mindful of the fact that I had been unimpressed by Mick Quinn and Brett Angell when I first saw them play, I advised:

"It's early days yet. Give the lad a chance."

No sooner had I uttered these words than Francis committed a really dirty foul – on himself. With a clear run at the Cardiff goal, he managed to hook one size thirteen boot around his other leg, floundered about for a second or two and toppled over like a huge tree.

"We're stuck with him anyway," I said in my defence.

"A cross between Keith Alexander and Bambi on ice." The comment came from someone behind me.

After this somewhat inauspicious home debut, Francis made way for the fit again Paul A Williams. Jason Lee's wage demands (or those of his agent) were at variance with what County were prepared to offer and he moved on to Lincoln City. A 1-0 defeat at leaders Darlington then placed County's promotion hopes in further jeopardy. It was at this stage that the manager made two more inspired adjustments to the make up of the team. Steve Bullock had certainly not let County down in the left-back role he had been asked to play all season. However, he was more at home in the centre of defence or on the right. Bergara's ploy was to recall left winger Paul R Williams, displaced from the side by Andy Kilner, to play at left-back. "Lionel" immediately looked as though he had played there all his career. The manager's second move was to recall Neil Matthews to play up front alongside the other Paul Williams.

Matthews scored both goals in the 2-2 home draw with Scarborough and played very well. Unfortunately, on the whole, the team didn't. This match,however, proved to be a turning point. Matthews, out of the side for much of the season, accepted gratefully the opportunity to show what he could do and Paul A Williams started to score regularly once more. A 3-2 win at Maidstone was followed by a 4-2 home win over Hereford, with Kilner claiming another couple of goals. A valuable point was gained in the next match away to promotion rivals Peterborough. It was at this point that we learned that County had accepted West Brom's offer of £250,000 for Paul A Williams. The big forward signed out with another goal in the 3-0 win over Rochdale. Kevin Francis came on as substitute in this match and looked a better player than he had done against Cardiff. Both he and his manager had obviously put in some hard work during the intervening month.

Good Friday heralded a six pointer against Hartlepool. Paul A Williams came on to the pitch to wave farewell to the fans. He received a great ovation. Signed as a centre half on a free transfer, he had proved himself to be one of the most effective forwards in the division. This transfer was the first of several major pay days that Danny Bergara was to provide for the club. Williams left Edgeley Park a hero but, unfortunately, he was soon to become an anti-hero at the Hawthorns where his missed penalty was to be a major factor in West Brom's relegation. For the match against Hartlepool his place was taken by Kevin Francis.

County played some superb football and, throughout the game it was one-way traffic towards the Hartlepool goal. Incredibly, due to a tenacious performance by the Hartlepool team in general, the goalkeeping heroics of Kevin Poole and the striking ability of Joe Allon, County found themselves 2-0 down. They left the field at half time to a standing ovation – the only time I can remember this happening with the result being as it was. The pattern of the second half was much the same as the first. Another breakaway and it was 3-0. Chris Beaumont reduced the arrears with a superb shot from the edge of the area. There were further near misses but no more goals. Again, County left the field with the crowd showing great appreciation. It had been a marvellous match with County playing most of the football but their opponents showing a blend of grit and opportunism that won the day. The new centre-forward was always a danger but, perhaps through being over-eager, managed to miss one or two chances.

A 1-0 defeat at Doncaster the following Monday completed County's miserable Easter and their promotion prospects were again looking a bit shaky. Whatever work went on behind the scenes between then and the following Saturday, it certainly seemed to do the trick. A 3-1 win over Chesterfield was sweet revenge for the mauling received at Saltergate the previous May. Neil Matthews scored the first of the ten goals that he was to score in the remaining nine games, making the game safe after County had led 2-1 with goals from Kilner and Beaumont.

The following Tuesday, County entertained Northampton and took the lead through Kevin Francis, his first goal after seven appearances in a County shirt. The obvious delight of the big man transmitted itself to the crowd and, from that moment on, he became a "cult" figure. Another goal from Matthews completed the scoring.

Consecutive 3-1 away wins at Gillingham and Wrexham meant that County were really back in business. Francis had learned to head the ball down instead of up and was becoming a real threat to opposing defences.

The next team to visit Edgeley was Aldershot on a warm Friday evening in mid April. When the names of the teams were read out on County's much improved public address system (for about 20 years nobody on the Pop Side had been able to hear a word), Aldershot's Mark Ogley was applauded by the home fans simply because he was the son of the former County goalkeeper. It was this match when the jitters started to creep in. Aldershot were looking the better team and Ogley was in danger of becoming much less popular than his dad, as the Hampshire side began to dominate the midfield exchanges. Typical of the way things were going was when Kevin Francis got his head to one of Kilner's missiles and effected a superb clearance to put Aldershot on the attack.

Dave Redfern had replaced the injured Paul Cooper in goal and, in spite of the occasional moment of eccentricity, had been playing very well. Against Aldershot that night he had a superb match as County managed to overcome their nerves and win 3-2. I have a mental picture of Redfern in the goal at the Cheadle End diving on top of the ball on the six yard line to put an end to a frantic scramble in the dying seconds of the game.

County then went on to beat Torquay 2-1 with Andy Kilner's goal of the season turning out to be the winner. As David Frain's magnificent crossfield pass bounced just nicely for him, the fans on the Pop Side could see that it was a goal the moment his boot made contact with the ball. Another narrow victory over opponents who would be promoted eventually via the play-offs.

Three matches remained and the jitters continued. At Blackpool, goals from Alan Finley and Jim Gannon were not enough to prevent defeat. 9000 fans saw that match.

And so to York for another fathers' and sons' outing which did not begin very auspiciously.

I forgot the sandwiches.

Heavy traffic on the M62 meant that we didn't have time to stop for anything.

Upon our eventual arrival at Bootham Crescent at about 2.30, feeling absolutely famished, I "treated" Craig, Tim and myself to some beef-burgers which should have carried a government health warning. I could still taste mine when I was negotiating the 80-mph dodgems at the Worsley interchange later that evening.

As for the match, it was a fairly drab affair but with the right result, two second half goals from Andy Kilner settling the issue.

The situation was now that County had to beat Scunthorpe, themselves play-off contenders, in the last match of the season at Edgeley Park, in order to ensure automatic promotion. Anything less and the dreaded play-offs would have to be encountered once again.

6,212 fans packed themselves into the then 8,000 capacity stadium to watch the showdown. I must admit that I expected a jittery nerve-jangling ninety minutes with County clinging desperately to a 1-0 lead or attempting to equalise with similar desperation. The lines on my forehead quickly disappeared as Beaumont's shot was blocked and Matthews fired in the rebound. After about fifteen minutes, County went two up through the by now immensely popular Kevin Francis. A fine save from Redfern ensured that the score at half-time remained 2-0. 2-1 at that stage could have altered the whole course of the match. I can't remember the order in which the three second half goals came. However, I recall a newspaper photograph of Kevin's second goal. Off balance as the ball is entering the goal, his foot appears to be higher than the crossbar. A law of perspective? Probably not.

Neil Matthews' second goal was of the type to thoroughly offend soccer purists. Route 1 "par excellence". A huge punt upfield by Redfern and Matthews headed the bouncing ball over the keeper. One second the ball was in the hands of the County keeper and the next second it was in the back of the Scunthorpe net. The passing game? Who needs it?

I am unsure of the order in which those goals came but I do remember that Alan "Il Supremo" Finlay got the fifth. This goal also contained its fair share of brute force, Finlay's forehead connecting with Kilner's massive throw to send the fans absolutely crazy. For those in my age group it was a day we had dreamed of for twenty-one years. All those horrendous drubbings sustained at the hands of Rochdale, Halifax, Hartlepool, Aldershot etc were a dim and distant memory. It must have been a wonderful moment for captain, Andy Thorpe, who had been there attempting valiantly to stem the tide in many of those matches. Brendan Ellwood went and took a bath, somewhat earlier than he had intended, a certain South American gentleman had a smile as wide as the estuary of the River Plate and, leaving Edgeley Park somewhat later than usual, I went to buy a "Football Pink".

1991-92

As County prepared for life back in the division that they had vacated so ignominiously in 1970, the manager began to become seriously architectural with his comments in the press and his notes in the club programme. Having laid the foundations of his bungalow, he was now seeking to add a conservatory before going on to construct a five-bedroomed detached in the stockbroker belt.

Since we had last witnessed a Division 3 match at Edgeley, the world had become a different place. The USSR and the Berlin Wall no longer existed. We had had Watergate, Irangate, Squidgygate and Countyslowestevergate. Nations had progressed from dictatorship to democracy and vice versa. Tyrants had slaughtered and been slaughtered in return. Technology had advanced at an awesome pace. The only real constant in the world had been Stockport County who had rarely ventured out of the bottom six of Division 4. Yes, it had been a long absence.

As is often the case, the first match of the season was played in glorious sunshine with the beautiful weather adding to the pleasure of seeing County repeat the score of the previous May, with Swansea City as their victims this time.

Apart from three heavy defeats – at Birmingham (0-3) and inexplicably bad displays at home to Chester City (0-4) and Shrewsbury Town (1-4) – County kept up a consistent level of performance and remained constantly in the top six. Some excellent results spring to mind. Home wins over Bradford (4-1), Peterborough (3-0) were the pre Christmas highlights, as was a 2-2 draw at Stoke where Mark Lillis, on his debut, and Kevin Francis, scored in the last ten minutes.

In September, Neil Edwards was signed from Leeds for a small fee and he made his debut against Bury in a match which County eventually won 2-0, Francis and Gannon scoring in the last few minutes. This match was notable for the performances of both goalkeepers. Kelly, for Bury, performed heroics while Edwards quickly became a favourite with the fans with a similar display at the opposite end of the pitch.

Another notable addition to the County ranks took place about half-way through the season when, once more, Danny Bergara, signed a forward of somewhat dubious pedigree. Andy Preece came from Wrexham for £10,000, having scored just eight times in fifty-one games for the Welsh club. Preece quickly developed a good understanding with Kevin Francis and his scoring rate in just over one hundred games for County was to be one every two games. I think that it is good when football fans salute a former player in recognition of what he gave to them. When Andy Preece appeared as substitute for Bury towards the end of the 1998-99 season, no doubt expecting to hear chants of "County reject", he appeared to be as surprised as he was chuffed by the warm reception that he received. (That was the only decent moment in an abysmal 0-0 draw).

In a season of "Oh so nearlys", many players were outstanding. Edwards and Preece played major roles, as did big Kevin, the promising Tony Barrass, Lee Todd, Chris Beaumont, David Frain, Peter Ward, Andy Thorpe and Bill Williams. However, this season belonged to Jim Gannon.

A target for a section of the crowd to begin with, Jim still had his detractors even after the promotion season. Convinced that his best position was in the centre of defence and, allegedly, at loggerheads with his manager over the midfield role that he was being asked to play, he nevertheless succeeded in becoming County's most effective player. Gannon helped himself to two hat-tricks, the first in the 3-0 Autoglass victory over York City, which enabled County to progress beyond the preliminary round in spite of a disastrous 4-0 defeat at Carlisle, where "Lionel" Williams sustained a broken leg.

His second hat-trick came in a memorable 4-1 win over Exeter. With about ten minutes remaining, the score was 1-1 when a slight altercation occurred between Preece and the Exeter keeper. The latter was shown a yellow card and he and his manager completely "lost it". Preece then compounded the felony by putting County 2-1 up. Gannon added his second and County's third before the home team were awarded a dubious penalty. The increasingly irate custodian saved Jim's first attempt but was adjudged to have moved illegally as the kick was about to be taken. He then said something to the referee along the lines of:

"I say, my dear fellow, I simply cannot bring myself to agree with that decision." – and was promptly shown a red card. Alan Ball was moved to express his own displeasure at this disciplinary action and, since it was a Friday night, we were in danger of finding the pubs shut before the penalty could be retaken. Fortunately, Gannon was allowed to dispatch the kick past the substitute goalkeeper and we made it to the pub with about an hour to spare.

A few weeks earlier, another Jim Gannon penalty had seriously curtailed drinking time in the 5-0 win over Bournemouth. This was the occasion when the floodlights conked out as he was about to take the kick and the teams had to leave the field for about half an hour. I can't remember what the exact score was at the time of the power cut, except that County had a comfortable lead. Not unnaturally, Bournemouth suggested that the match should be abandoned. This outcome was thwarted by a competent electrician. The penalty was put away eventually, also with competence. This must surely be another record. The longest time taken to score from a penalty?

Gannon was also a hero in the second leg of the Northern Section final of the Autoglass competition, his goal knocking the spirit out of Burnley and earning County their first-ever trip to Wembley.

Stoke City and Peterborough United, with a little help from Mark Stein, Ken Charlery and Martin Bodenham, saw to it that it all ended in tears.

1992-93

If 1991-92 belonged to Jim Gannon, then the man of this season was undoubtedly Kevin Francis. The big man had worked very hard to improve his overall style of play. Both his scoring ability and his control had improved considerably and his very presence was a constant menace to opposing defences.

In the goalscoring stakes, Kevin was aided and abetted by Gannon once more, Preece and Beaumont who between them managed to score over forty goals. But it was Francis who was to steal the limelight with a total of 39 goals from the league and the three cup competitions in which County were involved.

The season gave rise to plenty of goals and some very entertaining matches. The only cause for frustration was a loss of form towards the end of the season when a good run of results could well have seen automatic promotion achieved.

In the first half of the season, we were treated to some fine entertainment – a 5-3 home win over the then leaders, Hull City, in which County led 4-1 after 20 minutes, and convincing away victories at

Bradford (3-2) and Chester (3-0). These three consecutive victories were followed by a bit of a slump and a temporary stem in the flow of goals – three draws and two defeats with only Peter Ward's goal in the 1-1 home draw with Swansea to show for seven and a half hours' endeavour. It was with a feeling of foreboding, therefore, that I set out for the Friday evening fixture against Huddersfield Town on 30 October 1992. It was a crisp night and, en route to the home of football, it didn't take me long to realise that the heater in my car was not working properly. One glance at the temperature gauge and I knew that I had problems. I had to pull up, wait for the engine to cool down and then replace the frayed fan belt. This meant that I arrived at the ground about five minutes before half time. I was informed by the turnstile attendant that the score was 0-0 and that County were having the worst of what was a fairly poor match.

However, as I was walking through the Cheadle End towards my normal habitat on the pop side, I was greeted by the sight of Andy Preece nodding the ball into the Huddersfield net. Shortly after the celebrations had died down, half time arrived and I joined my pals to listen to a fair amount of moaning about the performance so far and learned from the general remarks that County were rather lucky to be a goal to the good.

"Did you see the goal?" I was asked.

"Yes." I replied. "They were just waiting for me to get here. I expect that the second half will be a vast improvement and that we will win easily."

"Bollocks." That was the general reaction to my somewhat bombastic forecast.

I spent the next 45 minutes gloating insufferably as County went on to win 5-0.

"Try and see if you can break down on the way to the next match," was the elated response from my associates.

It was to be some time before this happened to me again. However, on a gloomy Saturday afternoon in November 1997, the atrophied clutch on my ramshackle Fiat just lasted long enough to transport us to Edgeley in time for County's first league match against City since the year dot.

The defeat of Huddersfield was followed by a 3-0 win over Preston and a 2-0 defeat at Brighton. This inability to overcome sides who were struggling near the foot of the table was to cost County dearly in the spring of 1993.

In the League Cup, after seeing off Chester in the first round, they had played extremely well in the two matches against Nottingham Forest, losing both matches narrowly (3-2 and 2-1). Brian Clough was quoted as saying, "Stockport have some very good players, including one chap who could clean my upstairs windows without needing to use a ladder,"

In the FA Cup, County progressed to the Third Round with away victories at York City (3-1) and Macclesfield Town (2-0) on a pitch that was so sodden that, whenever the ball was kicked up in the air, it came down to earth with a plop and a squelch and hardly bounced at all. The reward for this victory was yet another away match, this time at the home of Derby County. 2 January 1993 is not a day of which I have very fond memories. We went over to Derby in a convoy of cars. The weather conditions were atrocious – very cold and very foggy. However, we were certain that the match would take place because the Baseball Ground, like the pitches of most clubs in the top flight, had undersoil heating. What a pity!

What a pity also that we didn't have a collection of umbrellas with us to protect us from the spittle that descended from the upper tier of the side into which the away fans were herded like bovine morons. Even without the fog, we wouldn't have been able to see much either, such was the appalling standard of the facilities for viewing the game. I haven't been to a match at Derby since then and I sincerely hope that Pride Park is an improvement upon the Baseball Ground.

After a largely unimpressive performance, County were trailing 1-0 with minutes remaining when Brian McCord who had joined County from Barnsley shortly before Christmas, popped up in the Derby penalty area to head the equaliser. (Derby were defending the end which was visible to us). Time to celebrate – the journey home through those appalling conditions would be worthwhile if we could get a replay out of it and be able to enjoy the rare luxury of an FA Cup tie taking place at Edgeley Park. It was while I was considering this prospect that a roar from the Derby fans told me that something was not quite right. It transpired that David Miller had done the home team an immense favour by heading them into Round 4. To be fair, he did atone to a certain extent the following week, by scoring for County in the 2-2 draw with Bradford. McCord, of course, who had been quite impressive in his short time with County was to have his career cruelly terminated some two months later by an awful tackle in a match at Swansea.

February was to prove an eventful and largely successful month, although this particular Lord Mayor's show was to be followed by a couple of quite sizeable muck carts. A comfortable 3-0 win over Wigan whetted the appetite for the visit of Bolton Wanderers, the eventual champions. County played superbly and won 2-0 with Preece and Francis scoring. A 2-2 draw at Exeter was followed by another excellent performance when County beat the division's "form" team, Port Vale, 2-0. I may be mistaken but I have a feeling that this was Vale's last defeat until they lost to West Brom in the final play-off match at Wembley. As for West Brom, they were the next visitors to Edgeley Park and played the role of "fall guys" in an astonishing match.

Paul A. Williams had returned to Edgeley Park for about one tenth of the amount that Bobby Gould had paid for his services and it was evident, as "Willow" took his place on the substitutes' bench, that he was not the flavour of this or any other month with the Baggies' fans. Gale force conditions had returned to Edgeley and, of course, there was no big edifice at the Cheadle End to act as a buffer, although West Brom fans were calling Williams a big edifice, or words to that effect. Conditions were such that the name of Billy Bocking was mentioned by one or two people near to me. This referred to the infamous decision of the County captain to play against a howling gale in the first half of the Fifth Round FA Cup tie against West Brom in the 1930s. It is the only time in County's history that they have found themselves 5-0 down at half time. However, acting captain, Jim Gannon, was having none of that and, having won the toss, decided that West Brom would battle against the elements in the first half. This they did to good effect.

In the West Brom team that fateful day was a quite talented though somewhat irascible character called David Speedie. (We had first encountered him playing for Darlington when he had lived up to his name and caused us all sorts of problems). County, with the wind behind them, were finding the conditions much more problematical than West Brom and it was no surprise when the visitors took the lead. At this stage of the match the only entertainment afforded to County fans was the barracking of Speedie, as the latter argued with every decision that did not go his way. Just before half time, Speedie was caught offside, threw his toys out of his pram and was shown a yellow card. Much mirth and merriment on the pop side gave way to great elation as, from the ensuing free kick, Jim Gannon scrambled home the equaliser.

During the interval, the euphoria caused by Gannon's goal subsided, to be replaced by a pessimistic feeling. The wind was showing no sign of abating and County were without two regular midfielders, David Frain and Peter Ward. However, in the second half, West Brom experienced the same problems as County had in the first. Sensibly, County played the ball about on the ground. (Something they were quite capable of in spite of the rubbish spouted by ITV commentators). Brian McCord and Jim Carstairs, in an unaccustomed role, started to control play in midfield and Chris Beaumont, playing wide on the left proceeded to have, in my opinion, his best 45 minutes in a County shirt. He set up a second goal for Gannon and then, making intelligent use of the conditions, sent over a low cross from the left with the outside of his right foot, swerving the ball directly into the path of the oncoming Kevin Francis who swept it imperiously into the net.

It was at this stage that Andy Preece appeared to be struggling with an injury. His obvious replacement decided to "warm up" in the vicinity of the Railway End. This served also to warm up the West Brom fans, whose displeasure at the way things were going and at the smile on the face of County's latest signing, was by then reaching Gargantuan proportions. Our friend, Mr. Speedie was not enjoying his afternoon and was substituted before he was sent off, much to his (and our) dismay. It is fairly safe to say that, when Williams eventually replaced Preece, he received something of a mixed reception.

Jim Carstairs capped a fine performance by making the score 4-1 and, by that time, it had become obvious that, if County were going to add a fifth goal, it would be made by Beaumont and scored by ...

West Brom fans were to have a triumphant end to the season but that afternoon must have been as much fun as listening to a Party Political Broadcast.

The following Tuesday County were due to play Chesterfield in the Northern semi-final of the Autoglass Trophy, a match which caused me a bit of apprehension, since County had already beaten the Derbyshire side 3-0 in the Preliminary Round the previous December. (Memories of the disaster at Carlisle and the ensuing revenge).

If the West Brom game, with its Wagnerian backdrop, could be construed as high drama, the Autoglass tie had all the ingredients of a tragi-comedy. Firstly, it might be appropriate to list the protagonists in the entertainment which was about to unfold.

Paul A. Williams – Forward (Stockport County). Having recently returned to the club from his disastrous sojourn at the Hawthorns and frustrated at his inability to attain his former goal scoring touch, he was in the frame of mind whereby he could start a punch up in an empty house.

Fred Barber – Goalkeeper (Chesterfield). Much travelled custodian who had opposed County on several occasions, most notably at Wembley when he did his best to redress the wrong done to us by Martin Bodenham and a Russian type linesman. For reasons best known to himself, he had adopted the rather strange habit of running out on to the field wearing a Halloween-type mask.

Greg Fee – Defender (Chesterfield). On loan to Chesterfield from Mansfield Town and a player whom Danny Bergara had tried to sign from Sheffield Wednesday three or four years earlier. At the time County couldn't afford the fee. (Ugh!).

I have mentioned my foreboding and was not surprised, therefore, when Chesterfield took the lead early in the game. Although Williams himself equalised just before half time, County were unable to make second half pressure count. As the game wore on, it looked as though it would be a case of a penalty shoot-out. Indeed, this appeared to be Chesterfield's aim as there was quite a lot of time wasting, with a fair amount of it perpetrated by their goalkeeper. As the end of the match approached, a Chesterfield player went down injured. In accordance with custom, the player in possession of the ball, in this case Barber, booted it into touch (about half way inside the Chesterfield half of the pitch).

After receiving attention, the player was able to carry on, apparently none the worse for wear. Williams went to take the throw-in. With everyone expecting him to concede possession back to Chesterfield, he hurled the ball into the penalty area. The outcome was a corner. Barber and his colleagues expressed their displeasure at this unsporting action in no uncertain terms. There ensued quite an entertaining few minutes of what cricketers refer to as "sledging" and Chesterfield fans chanting "Cheat".

When the corner was eventually taken and Kevin Francis scored from it, there was more sledging than on the slopes of Lyme Park.

Barber raced out of his goal to remonstrate with the referee and the celebrating Paul Williams. His face was so contorted with rage that a voice behind me urged:

"Put your mask on, Fred, you're frightening all the kids!"

Apparently, the angst of the Chesterfield players continued long after the match had finished. The story was that they had booted in the door of their dressing room, probably wishing it was Paul Williams' head.

Now, where does Mr. Fee fit into all this? Well, he had spent the evening defending against all that County could throw at him and his colleagues. As a player who was only on loan to the Derbyshire club, he was probably not one of those who decided that the dressing room door needed replacing. When County entertained bottom of the league Mansfield the following Friday, who should run out to face Kevin Francis again? Yes, that's right, Greg Fee returned to Edgeley Park for the second time in a week. As I have said, this particular season, County failed to secure an automatic promotion position because of their inability to beat teams in the bottom six. Shortly to be relegated, Mansfield duly completed the double over County, winning 1-0 in a match which was very similar in pattern to that of the previous Tuesday. The only difference was that County were short of a couple of goals and Greg Fee, having stood up defiantly to two Kevin Francis-inspired onslaughts in the space of four days, walked off Edgeley Park battered and bruised but having exacted a revenge comparable to that of the Count of Monte Cristo. You would have to be a particularly bigoted and biased County fan to begrudge him that moment of triumph – and we all did, of course.

And Paul Williams? His next act of note was to be sent off for thumping the Swansea player who clobbered Brian McCord. As the season approached the final stages, things were not ever so pleasant.

As the transfer deadline approached, Danny Bergara became rather busy. This was after the 2-2 draw at Swansea, a 2-1 defeat at Stoke, yet another unpleasant affair which culminated in the incident with Jim Gannon and Mark Stein, and an awful 0-0 draw at home to lowly Brighton.

Peter Duffield was signed on loan from Sheffield United and started in sensational fashion with two goals in a 3-2 win at Preston and two more the following Tuesday when County defeated Hartlepool 4-1. Unfortunately, he didn't score any more for us.

Two players were signed from Preston – Martin James and Mike Flynn. Rumour had it that Danny had asked Kevin Francis which centre half he found the most difficult to play against. The reply was "Flynn". If this rumour is true, then it was a very shrewd question to ask and one which met with an excellent answer. At the time the £125,000 spent on Flynn was the club's record transfer pay out. Even so, it must go down as the bargain of the 1990s.

Kevin celebrated his advisory role with a hat-trick in the 4-3 win at Plymouth, a match in which on loan goalkeeper, Phil Kite, made his debut, replacing Neil Edwards. Another rumour was rife, namely that Edwards was being disciplined because of an incident at the club's annual dinner at the Acton Court Hotel. The other aspect of the rumour was that, to celebrate the arrival of Mike Flynn, somebody had slipped Edwards a Micky Finn!

I remember seeing Kite play on TV during Bristol City's FA Cup run the previous season and he had looked to be a very good goalkeeper. Unfortunately, he didn't this time. Five matches and eleven goals later, Edwards was restored to his rightful position. With Flynn now established in the centre of the defence, the goals against column showed an immediate and marked improvement. The only problem was that County's free scoring forwards now ceased to score freely. At that stage, Kevin Francis had scored 37 times but, suspended for the play-off matches against Port Vale, he only managed another two. He scored the second goal in the 2-0 win over Wigan in the Autoglass Northern Final to give County another Wembley appearance and County's goal in the final itself. Individual fans will have varied opinions about what is County's finest hour, but there can be no doubt that this was County supporters' finest hour.

2-0 down at half time and being played off the pitch by Port Vale, it was a case of "Let's give it our best shot". The mood swept through the ranks and a non-stop barrage of noise helped to lift the team. Kevin's goal was also our goal but, in spite of a wall of sound that made Phil Spector's efforts look like a picket fence, neither Kevin nor the fans could repeat the performance. We had been pipped at the post once again – but at least we felt that we had achieved something. I think it was the least depressing of my return journeys from Wembley.

1993-94

Whether the self-belief was already there or whether it had been re-instilled by the manager, County certainly had plenty of it as they put behind them the disappointment of the previous May, making a superb start to the new season.

However, the air of the North East coast must not have suited them because the only blemishes on the excellent start were the two defeats at Hartlepool, 1-0 in the league and 2-1 in whatever the League Cup called itself at that time. Otherwise it was all systems go with plenty of goals. Darren Ryan had joined County from Chester City in an exchange deal involving Paul Wheeler. Although Wheeler had been a useful player and had scored some important goals, looking quite impressive in his limited number of first team opportunities, it looked for a while at least that County had got the best of the deal. A skilful and speedy winger, Ryan was also aware of the location of the goal posts, scoring seven times in a seventeen match run which was ended by injury. For some reason, his opportunities were very limited afterwards.

After fifteen matches, County led the league with a record that was practically the opposite of their start to the 1986-87 season.

Played: 15. Won: 11. Drawn: 3. Lost: 1. For: 32. Against: 10. Points: 36

As well as Ryan, Andy Preece had started the season in fine form, so much so that, at that stage, he was scoring more frequently than Kevin Francis who had found the net nine times. Preece had managed thirteen and this gave us some cause for concern. In his previous one and a half seasons at County, he had scored this unlucky number of goals and had then suffered injury. A hat-trick against Swansea on 30 October saw him arrive at this total. He must have felt as relieved as he was delighted when his injury time winner at Rotherham put County into the second round of the FA Cup after they had been 1-0 down after 85 minutes.

As County swept aside most of the opposition in the autumn of 1993, it became time to start the refurbishment of the Barlow Stand, aka the Pop Side. And so, on 16 October, for the visit of Alan Ball's struggling Exeter side, exiled from our half way line haven, we took our places in the small enclosure behind the Cheadle End goal. It was from this point that you got a goalkeeper's eye view of Kevin Francis. What an awesome sight that was! I wouldn't dive at that guy's size thirteen feet even with a crash helmet on. In fact Exeter's Vesey bravely attempted just that,as with the game just a few minutes old, Francis raced through the defence, avoided the keeper's dive and tucked the ball into the corner of the net. County went on to win 4-0, with this effort supplemented by goals from Darren Ryan, David Frain and Peter Ward. The only surprise was that Preece failed to score.

However, the smaller of County's strike force, 6'4", duly obliged with a superb volley to provide us with a 1-0 win at Craven Cottage the following week. On 30 October, Swansea City were the visitors. Swansea were quickly on the wrong end of a penalty decision, with their midfielder, Warren Aspinall dismissed for keeping out a Kevin Francis header with a forearm jab. As Jim Gannon was sitting on the substitutes' bench, the penalty was taken by the taller of County's deadly duo. To everyone's surprise he placed the ball skilfully into the corner of the net instead of, as had been speculated, booting it a la Charlie McDonnell on to the railway lines. Swansea were extremely upset about the decision and the outcome, although Aspinall had clearly handled the ball on the line and, in accordance with the rules, had to go. A constant barrage of moaning at the referee and linesmen resulted in a couple of bookings before Andy Preece added insult to injury by scoring at the start of the second half. It all became too much for Roger Freestone in the Swansea goal and he too was shown a yellow card for a comment made to the referee. Doing more grumbling than Victor Meldrew, Freestone appeared to be on the point of receiving a different coloured card when a voice from behind me bellowed, "You'll be blaming the referee for your bed wetting problem, next!"

Having heard the comment quite clearly, the referee, struggling to keep a straight face, turned away and put his cards back into his pocket. I am sure that this remark saved Swansea from having to play the rest of the match with nine men. When everyone got back to playing football, Andy Preece completed a superb hat-trick.

A bad run of form towards the end of the year meant that, by Christmas, County had surrendered the leadership to Reading. Over the holiday period, they lost 2-0 to the new leaders. However, a 5-1 defeat of now non-league Halifax in the second round had set up a third round tie against Premiership aristocrats (yes, that's right) Queen's Park Rangers. Gerry Francis' side had several famous names, the most notable being the current England centre-forward, Les Ferdinand and former England midfielder, Ray Wilkins.

I remember having to queue for tickets on a bitterly cold day just before Christmas – typical of the suffering that most fans endure in the support of their team. There was quite a lot of moaning and whingeing, though most of it was good humoured.

Now, talking of whingeing, that brings me back to the ex England midfielder due to lead his colleagues in this third round tie. Wilkins, although in the twilight of his career, was still a very good player as his display at Edgeley Park proved. Some say, unkindly perhaps, that he was not a good player for England or, even more unkindly, that he produced more square balls than Salvador Dali. However, one thing is certain – he was good enough to whinge for England.

8 January 1994 dawned bright and frosty and the Edgeley Park pitch, affected as it was by faulty drainage after the refurbishment of our sadly missed terracing, was hard, though not rutted, as some of the QPR contingent have claimed.

"Not fit to play on!" wailed Wilkins.

"Bollocks.".said referee John Key.

"We can't be expected to play on that!" moaned Gerry Francis.

"It's the same for both teams," said Danny Bergara, "and it's just like the lawn behind the splendid detached residence that I am in the process of building."

"That's an even bigger load of bollocks." said the referee.

And so the match took place. After about fifteen minutes, a low drive from Simon Barker put the Londoners in front. Les Ferdinand missed a fairly easy chance to add to the lead before Kevin Francis equalised with another superbly placed low shot as County's Tony Barrass lay injured in an offside position.

"Offside ref!" shouted Wilkins, as he tugged at the official's sleeve.

"Bollocks," said Key.

"Can't you say anything else apart from 'bollocks'? You rude, inarticulate, incompetent official." protested the QPR spokesman.

"Yes. This is a yellow card and I'm showing it to you, you whingeing git. Now, what's your name?"

"Er, Trevor Francis,"

"Don't try and work that old Mossman scam on me. You might have been moaning all match but you haven't burst into tears once. What's your real name?"

The teams went in all square at half time. In the second half, the temperature dropped and the tempo increased. Then came the cleverly lobbed free kick from Peter Ward which was volleyed brilliantly into the net by Andy Preece. Of course, Preece would never have got to the ball if Darren Peacock had not slipped on the treacherous surface (either that or Kevin Francis was standing on his hair).

In any event, Wilkins and Francis (Gerry, that is) must have enjoyed the result of the fourth round match against Bristol City. Having put one over on Liverpool, they put four over on County. Initially, I was most upset because a professional commitment prevented me from going to that match. (It had been postponed from the Saturday). My daughter Sian had the dubious pleasure of using my ticket. She still hasn't given me the money for it.

Oh well, now we can concentrate on the league. Fortress Edgeley, breached only once in 1992-93 (by bottom club Mansfield), was now starting to look more like a sandcastle, probably due to the fact that the pitch resembled a beach. Some dodgy home performances were giving us some cause for concern. Prior to the Bristol match, Fulham had gone away with three points courtesy of a 4-2 victory, with two of their goals coming from a certain Jeff Eckhardt.

Neil Edwards sustained a nasty shoulder injury that would keep him out for the rest of the season and his place was taken, firstly by Ian Ironside, and then by John Keeley, as the manager strove to tighten up the defence. With Bill Williams still unavailable, David Miller was moved back from midfield to play alongside Mike Flynn, leaving Jim Gannon probably somewhat disgruntled at having to continue in midfield. The ploy worked well for a while at least, as a useful 1-1 draw away to "form" team Port Vale was followed by impressive home wins over Hartlepool (5-0) and Huddersfield (3-0). "Edgar" Wallace scored the winner at Wrexham and an Andy Preece goal secured a point from a tough match at Burnley. Three wins and two draws – back on track? Not really – a 2-1 win at Rotherham was sandwiched between two more home defeats. York City won 2-1 and the next visitors, Bournemouth, who must have been quite apprehensive when they saw the name of Cantona in the County squad. It wasn't Eric, of course, but his brother Joel. Oooh, aah, 2-0 to Bournemouth – aah.

And so, it looked like the play-offs would be County's lot once again, although there were a couple of highlights that emerged from a fairly erratic run. County beat Brentford 3-1 in an entertaining match, with two more from good old Kevin who repeated the feat against Port Vale in the next match. Vale had risen from mid table at Christmas to lie just behind Reading in second place. The highlight, and the most terrifying moment, of this match was when Bill Williams, having just returned from injury, suddenly found himself with the ball at his feet in his own penalty area and hemmed in by a crowd of players from both sides. Williams, apparently oblivious to the fact that County were leading by just the one goal and that this most important of matches was nearing its close, coolly dribbled the ball past three opponents and one of his own team mates before emerging from the penalty area to set up a counter attack. I don't think any other player could have got away with it.

Postponements, caused by the dire condition of the pitch, meant that County had to play three games in a week in late April. As the last of these matches was at home to leaders Reading, they did well to hold on for a draw, having led 1-0 for much of the match. In actual fact County managed to avoid defeat in the last ten league games. The only problem was that six of them were drawn. Indeed, they went to meet their arch-rivals, Burnley, and nemesis, Mr. Elleray, on the back of a twelve match unbeaten run. Chris Beaumont's goal (I was certain he was going to miss) saw off York City after a 0-0 draw at Bootham Crescent.

Much has been written about that infamous Wembley encounter and I think it is best to leave it at that – except to say that along with our other unenviable record held jointly with the Swiss national side, we are so far the only team ever to have two players sent off in a match there.

1994-95

All good things must come to an end, and the breaking up of the team that had never finished below sixth since the start of the decade was signalled by the departure of Andy Preece to the then Premiership Crystal Palace for a fee reported to be between £350,000 and £400,000, either figure representing an excellent profit on a player who had cost £10,000. Preece had averaged a goal every other game in his two and a half years at County.

Rumours also abounded that the other half of the nearly thirteen foot strike force would also be soon on his way to higher things. However, this did not deter the manager as it looked like business as usual for the "nearly" men who walloped Cardiff City 4-1 in the opening game of the season.

Impressive debuts were made by close season signings, Jeff

Eckhardt, Martyn Chalk and a young man signed from Newcastle for £35,000, Alun Armstrong. Alun marked his debut with a goal. Peter Ward and Kevin Francis (2) completed the scoring. Mike Flynn was sent off in the last minute of this match, having been the victim of a base act of skulduggery. Cardiff's Stant also received his marching orders and a deserved smack in the chops for doing to Flynn what Vinny Jones once did to Paul Gascoigne.

The popular Dean Emerson, making a welcome though too short return to County, was booked along with Martyn Chalk who, although looking to be quite a good player, seemed determined to spend half the season under suspension.

Apart from the disastrous first leg of the second round Coca-Cola Cup match against Sheffield United (What sweet revenge two years later), things were going really well and it seemed that another play-off place would be the least that County could expect.

When Matthew Bound made his debut in the 1-0 win at Leyton Orient, County had risen to second place. Francis and Armstrong were working out a good partnership and were scoring regularly. However, there were signs that one or two things were not quite right behind the scenes. Dean Emerson was the first to fall out of favour and his second spell at Edgeley Park was terminated rather abruptly. Goalkeeper John Keeley also departed quickly and quietly. Kevin Francis was injured in a 1-0 defeat at Chester, but not before he had managed to miss a penalty. November was disastrous as the goals dried up completely. A 1-0 First Round FA Cup exit at Wrexham came amid two 2-0 defeats at the hands of Oxford United and Swansea City. On the last Saturday of November, Birmingham's 1-0 win at Edgeley saw County slide down to tenth place. This was Kevin's last full match for County as he was to join our opponents shortly afterwards for a fee reported to be in the region of £800,000. He was to treat us to just one more goal, returning from injury to come off the substitutes' bench and score in the 2-1 home defeat by Bradford City just before Christmas.

Without Kevin Francis as his partner, Alun Armstrong went through a very barren spell and even lost his place in the team.

In the new year, the signing of Ian Helliwell from Rotherham helped to bring about an improvement for a while. Helliwell, despite scoring twice on his debut in the 4-0 home win over Hull City, didn't score many more that season. However, his work rate and his unselfish willingness to put himself about had a beneficial effect upon his young partner who started to rediscover his form and his scoring touch.

Along with the previous November, February proved to be the worst spell of Danny Bergara's reign at Edgeley Park and a 4-0 defeat at Oxford saw County fall as low as sixteenth. March provided a bit of an improvement and a climb up to half way. However, an era was about to come to an end.

The fortune teller told Julius Caesar to "Beware the Ides of March". A similar character should have told County to "Beware the Acton Court Hotel". It was there at the club's annual knees-up where Danny Bergara might have said "Et tu, Brendan", as his tenure as manager of Stockport County ended in the most unsavoury manner imaginable. I prefer to make no comment regarding the rights or wrongs of the affair, but it was such a pity that it all had to end in that way.

And so, the man from Montevideo left for the last time the office where he had dreamed of becoming the first South American to lead out an English league club at Wembley.

Nevertheless, he had left the club quite a legacy. If a manager is to be judged by the service that he obtains from the players he signs or the amount of profit he makes in the transfer market, there can only be one verdict regarding Danny Bergara. Players whom he signed for nothing or for bargain prices still form the backbone of the team that is currently holding its own in Division 1. On the other hand, perhaps he had taken the club as far as he could and a fresh approach was needed.

The appointment of Dave Jones as his successor was something of a surprise. However, the new manager sorted things out quite competently in the short-term and the team finished fairly strongly in eleventh place. Another plus factor was the demise of those horrendously gaudy shirts that the team had worn ever since they had achieved promotion in 1991.

19

The Dirtiest Foul of Them All

As a totally biased football supporter, I have seen many dirty fouls committed against my team as they fought valiantly and fairly to achieve success against all odds.

This is not strictly true, of course. I can recall one Friday night in the early 1990s when Kevin Francis missed the ball completely and centred the Leyton Orient full back instead.

Nigel Batch's invitation to a Rotherham forward to join his team's supporters in watching the match from the Paddock was on a par with the infamous foul perpetrated by German goalkeeper Schumaker in the 1982 World Cup Finals which caused France's Batiston to postpone his wedding.

Perhaps the best documented foul of all time was when one Andoni Goicoechea, aka the Butcher of Bilbao, caused a certain Diego Armando Maradona to roll around most of the pitch, the Hand of God clutching his bruised bollocks. *(Must have been like a couple of King Edwards the next day. – Ed)*

However, when Alan "Il Supremo" Finley flattened a Chester City player in a match at Macclesfield, the poor guy couldn't roll around the pitch. He had been trodden into it!

Quite amazingly, the Football League allowed Chester to play for two seasons at the Moss Rose whilst they were in the process of moving from Sealand Road to the Diva Stadium. Then, in 1996, when Macc. Town won the Conference championship, their stadium was considered to be not quite up to the standard for admission to the Third Division. They had carried out the required improvements but had failed to meet the deadline for completing them and so were denied admission to the league. That has got to be the dirtiest foul of the lot.

20

A Tangled Wilderness and a 60-Year Dream

When the new Cheadle End stand was officially opened for the start of the 1995-96 season, Fortress Edgeley almost seemed to resemble a fortress. Our Premier League neighbours, Manchester City, had agreed to take part in the celebrations and a sweltering night at the end of July marked the grand opening.

The heat wave continued throughout August and it was never hotter than for the first home match of the season. The visitors were newly-relegated Burnley and their winger, Ted McMinn, was the recipient of lots of sweets. He didn't seem to appreciate very much the gifts that were being showered upon him. At least it was an improvement upon what Edgar Wallace had showered on him the last time the two clubs had met.

David Jones' first season in charge was a strange one. The main disappointment was the home form, particularly in the first half of the season. There were plenty of good points, however, including good performances in the two major cup competitions and an obvious change in the style of play. This came about with the acquisition in the first instance of Tom Bennett and, in the second half of the season, after Bennett had broken a bone in his foot in the cup tie at Everton, the arrival of Chris Marsden.

It was only when these two had the opportunity to complement each other's skills the following season that all the pieces of the jigsaw were to fall into place.

This was also the era of own goals. Tony Dinning was already known as "OG" by a section of the crowd, but his efforts were nowhere near as good as the two FA Cup own goals which made ideal curtain raisers to the Ian Dowie classic of the following season.

John Beck brought his struggling Lincoln City side to Stockport for the First Round of the FA Cup and County chalked up an easy 5-0 victory in what will be remembered mainly as "Jigsaw" Jeff Eckhardt's match. Apparently so called because of a propensity for "falling to pieces" in the opposition penalty area, Jigsaw scored a hat-trick and ended up in goal when Neil Edwards had to leave the field injured. However, County's fourth goal was an absolute gem.

As Lincoln pressed forward, Chris Beaumont found himself just inside his own half to be the nearest player to the Lincoln goal. As the ball was cleared upfield, Beaumont made a diagonal run towards the ball bisecting the half-way line as he did so. At the same time, the Lincoln goalkeeper raced from his goal and a defender raced back to try and beat Beaumont to the ball. Poor Chris had not scored for ages and he wasn't going to that day either. The defender whipped the ball off his toe to send a 45-yard back pass all along the ground and with unerring accuracy past his onrushing colleague.

John Beck's reaction to the 5-0 drubbing was to have his team run round the pitch after the match. This action seemed to serve no useful purpose other than to give his team the opportunity to trade insults with a group of departing County fans. The Second Round saw County drawn at home again (something which doesn't seem to happen these days), this time to Unibond League Blyth Spartans, who had beaten County in 1971 at the same stage of the competition. There was to be no upset this time as County were comfortable 2-0 winners. The second goal came about when a shot from Tom Bennett struck the post. In his attempts to avoid knocking the rebounding ball into his own net, a Blyth defender performed a series of dance steps rather like Mick Jagger used to do when the Stones performed "It's All Over Now". To no avail, his own goal meant that it was all over for Blyth Spartans for another year.

The Third Round tie at Everton gave rise to another unusual goal as well as a superb County performance. As County trailed 2-1, a brilliant crossfield pass from Lee Todd found Chris Beaumont out on the right. He crossed first time very hard and low. Ian Helliwell elected to head the ball rather than shoot although the ball must have been no more than six inches off the ground when he made contact. The startled Neville Southall could do nothing about it. There had been nothing unusual about County's first equaliser – a superb volley from Alun Armstrong. The replay, of course, saw the cup holders progress to Round Four in most dramatic and (for John Henshaw) painful fashion.

County also did well in the Coca-Cola Cup, playing Ipswich Town for the first time ever in the Second Round. County were not very impressive in the first leg at Edgeley Park, when a Martyn Chalk effort equalised an earlier free kick blast from Ipswich. The non-used substitute, Tony Dinning, was heard to remark after the match to his fellow Geordie, Alun Armstrong, "Ah had a better second half than yer!" In the second leg, County came back from 1-0 down to win 2-1, thanks to an extra time winner from Jim Gannon.

The Third Round proved to be the end of the trail for County, as a team weakened by injury lost 2-0 at Villa Park, with Edwards, Flynn, Gannon, Todd and Connelly putting up a fine defensive display. This ability to avoid being overwhelmed by teams from higher divisions was a foretaste of what was to come the following season.

This was the only time in my life that I have ever owned a County shirt, not that I'd ever hankered after one of those yucky Cobra Lager ones. However, this was much better – white with the blue pin stripes. It was a birthday present from my daughter. Unfortunately, because of her wicked sense of humour, the number on the back denoted my age. On a warm September afternoon at Shrewsbury, I removed my jacket to the amusement of the County fans behind me.

"Not even United have a squad with that number of players!" That was one of the kinder remarks as we cheerfully watched County win 2-1, somewhat against the run of play.

Neil Edwards had to play particularly well and was deservedly referred to as "Wales Number One", the same group of fans shouting across to the Shropshire supporters "You're not English, you're Welsh!"

The season finished on quite a high note, too, with a good run of results meaning that, on the last Saturday of the season, we still had a chance of a play-off place. A creditable 0-0 draw at promoted Swindon was not enough and County had to settle for a respectable ninth position. It had been a season of consolidation in the first instance, but there had been some good football played. The manager had also made some useful additions to the squad during the course of the campaign. He had managed to acquire the services of John Jeffers on a free transfer from Port Vale, Kieron Durkan from Wrexham, Chris Marsden from Notts County and Andy Mutch from Swindon to replace Ian Helliwell who had been transferred to Burnley. Mutch quickly elevated himself to cult status with a hat-trick in the 4-2 home win over promotion chasing Oxford. As Swindon and Oxford were the two leading clubs in the division that season, the local rivalry must have been even more intense than usual. Mutch, as a former Swindon player, received plenty of abuse from the Oxford fans and failed hopelessly to conceal his joy upon completion of his hat-trick. It was also good to see Oxford captain, Les Robinson, still going strong, and even better to see him finish on the losing side for once as County chalked up their first ever victory over Oxford.

Before and at the start of the next season, David Jones was to make some more very crucial signings. The contributions of Paul Jones, Luis Cavaco and the returning Brett Angell were vital to say the least, as was the eleventh hour role played by loan signing Kevin Cooper.

The season began on a note of sheer farce. Over the years, managers and coaches have provided us with many a laugh with excuses for the failure of their teams. A team that once lost to Southampton because they were wearing grey shirts is one that springs immediately to mind. However, I have every sympathy with the Birmingham City manager and his explanation of his team's 4-0 defeat in a pre-season friendly which took place either at the end of July or at the beginning of August. The grass was too long. And he was quite right.

The extent to which County were prepared to cheat to win this match was never more apparent than in the manner in which the first goal was scored. With the game about five minutes old, John Jeffers hid with the ball in a clump of elephant grass until a couple of defenders ran past. He then passed the ball to Cavaco who, being smaller than Bruce and Ablett was more able to weave his way through the tangled undergrowth to get in a shot at goal. The ball was beaten out to Andy Mutch who promptly scored. Although he had been standing for several minutes in an offside position, he was screened from the view of the linesman by a row of hollyhocks.

You had to feel sorry for the Birmingham manager. This sort of bad sportsmanship really goes against the grain. All together now, to the tune of "English Country Garden",

There is joy in July,
When Trevor starts to cry,
In County's wild life ga-arden.

Some ten months later, walking back to the car after County had clung on desperately to beat Wycombe Wanderers in about the 65th match of the season, my old mate Dave Booth, young Tim Hesketh and myself came unanimously to the conclusion that watching

County would never get any better than it had this season. County's battle weary men had finished the match on autopilot. "Playing from memory" is, I think, the way that Manager Jones described his team's performance. It was a good job that the memory of Goalkeeper Jones served to remind him that he was the best in the division, as he needed to be with the engines of most of his team mates in desperate need of a service.

Yet, it could all have ended so differently. With two draws and four defeats from the first six league games, County were in 23rd place and the manager's job was rumoured to be on the line. It was at that stage that Jones and several of his players sat down and had a very important cup of tea and discussed what was going wrong.

Jim Gannon, no doubt, would have had plenty to contribute to that discussion. He also had plenty to contribute to the next match, scoring twice in the 3-1 win over Plymouth Argyle, a match which was the turning point of the whole season. As well as Gannon's efforts and a superbly lobbed goal by Alun Armstrong, this match contained a remarkable piece of excellent football.

Shortly into the second half, Bruce Grobelaar raced out of his goal in a vain attempt to stop the ball from going for a corner. Kieron Durkan, realising that Grobelaar had a long way to go to get back to his position, took the corner immediately dropping the ball straight on to Brett Angell's head. Angell headed the ball down firmly in the opposite direction to which Grobelaar was running. Somehow, the ex- Liverpool man managed to twist in mid-air and pull off a remarkable save.

I shall just mention one or two highlights that have stuck very clearly in my memory because detailed events of this best ever season have been chronicled already by "The Tea Party" editor, David Espley, in his excellent "Saturday Night and Thursday Morning". What a season to choose when you promise yourself that you will watch every single match. He must have felt a bit sick round about 10 September, though!

One match which springs readily to mind, as County proceeded to lose just three of their next thirty matches, is that magnificent performance at Bramall Lane when Alun Armstrong proved beyond all doubt that he was a player of the highest class and his team mates showed us that County were a team that was definitely going places.

This led to the match at League Champions Blackburn where Chris Marsden, Mike Flynn and Paul Jones were particularly outstanding in a wonderful team performance and the two Tims, Sherwood and Flowers combined to produce another own goal of slapstick proportions – a fitting entrée to the magnificent soufflée soon to be served up by Mr. Dowie

In the league, the best performance in January was probably the 5-1 demolition of Millwall, in which Luis Cavaco scored twice and a certain former England international, now a member of the visitors' midfield, interrupted proceedings on several occasions to have a whinge about something.

March saw the return of Danny Bergara to his old stomping ground, in charge of relegation-bound Rotherham United. He received and acknowledged a fitting ovation from the fans and escaped with a point from a 0-0 draw, but only because a dozy official failed to notice a Rotherham defender practically mug Kieron Durkan just outside the six yard area.

That was one of four really bad refereeing performances I saw that season the others being:

* The sending off of Matthew Bound in the first leg of the Coca-Cola Cup tie against Chesterfield. Paul Jones chested the ball away as Bound had actually passed it back to him.
* Steve Bruce's refereeing of the Fourth Round FA Cup tie at St. Andrew's, where the grass was too short in any case
* The performance of our friend, Mr Elleray, in the first leg of the Coca-Cola Semi-Final.

The season progressed to its two climaxes with County's leg weary troops plodding gamely on whilst a certain manager, not too far away, in geographical terms at any rate, was complaining bitterly about the number of games that his team had to play.

Twenty-one cup ties later, after kicking off in that first leg against Chesterfield, County were left with no trophies, but a final lap to stagger into Division 1.

If someone had said to me in the autumn of 1986 that, in ten years time, a team that had cost over £30,000,000, including two Brazilian internationals and an Italian international, who was the premier league's leading goal scorer, would be doing a lap of honour to celebrate the fact that they had only lost 1-0 at home to Stockport County, I would have judged that person to be a certifiable lunatic who should be locked in a cell and left to play "Football Manager" at Level 1 on an outdated Amstrad computer. In actual fact, I was surprised that the Italian international was capable of doing a lap of honour. He had looked to be injured so badly in the incident that resulted in Tony Dinning being invited to go and run the bath water. His performance brought an offer from the Royal Shakespeare Company but, even after they had received a nice hand-out from the National Lottery, they couldn't afford his signing-on fee.

And so to Saltergate for the showdown between the two sets of cup heroes, or in my case to the car park opposite the Five Ways. I think we were right, Tim, Dave and I. Watching County won't ever be any better.

21

A Worthy Knight and a Portaloo

And so County were about to play their first match in the top half of the football league for sixty years. The last time they had been this high, the world had been an entirely different place. People had just about started to realise that Adolf Hitler was a threat to world peace, not to mention humanity, a civil war was raging in Spain, the United States was still in the grips of the Depression and beer was about 1d a pint.

The close season had been traumatic. David Jones, of course, had replaced Graeme Souness at Southampton and, soon afterwards, Paul Jones and Lee Todd had followed him to the south coast.

Gary Megson came from Blackpool and had to find some replacements straight away.

The start mirrored that of the previous season. Was this a good omen or a cause for concern? The former, it seemed, as an excellent run of form in October and November saw County climb steadily up the table. The highlight of this spell was the victory over City, of course. What good fun it was to be able to be patronising to City fans.

A fairly bad run from February through to Easter saw County drop down a bit but a late season improvement ensured that they finished in eighth position, the highest in the club's history. All things considered, it must be admitted that the manager had done well in his first season in charge.

Strangely enough, apart from the first half of the home match against Manchester City, the two most entertaining games were cup ties against teams from lower divisions. It seems strange to refer to Mansfield Town and Preston North End in those terms because they had both been above us for so long. Even when they had both sunk into the Fourth Division, they still used to come to Edgeley Park and give County what for. Mind you, most teams did in those days.

The 6-3 thriller in the second leg of the Coca-Cola Cup tie with Mansfield was indeed a match to savour, one of those matches that coaches hate and fans love. If this is what football is like in Division 3, let's go back there! No, please disregard that remark. It could happen!

It was very strange to be playing a league match when the First Round of the FA Cup was taking place. Preston had had to battle through the first two rounds to be rewarded with a glamour tie against a club from the higher echelons of the league!

The Third Round tie at Deepdale was played under the worst conditions possible – lashing rain and a gale force wind. As John Henshaw drove us at a fair rate up the M61, he had a job to hold the car steady as the vehicle was buffeted by frequent squally gusts. The conditions were very reminiscent of the time we had played Cambridge some ten years earlier. Incredibly, the rain stopped just as we reached Preston and we were able to get from parking space to ground without getting drenched.

Preston's most famous plumber had received a knighthood in the New Year's Honours List and the club had thought it appropriate to make a formal presentation to him before the tie. Such was the force of the gale that the red carpet laid down upon the Deepdale mud was blown half the length of the pitch towards the end that Preston would be defending in the first half. Eventually, someone had the bright idea of having the ball boys stand on the edge of the carpet to stop it blowing away and the ceremony went ahead without hitch. It was good to hear both sets of fans giving a tremendous ovation to a man who had served both club and country with such distinction.

I trust that the company owned by the worthy knight had nothing to do with the lavatorial facilities at the disposal of away supporters. Now I know that County's'record in this area has been far from a shining example over the years, the antiquated and rudimentary facilities on the Pop Side were for many years usable only for the absolutely desperate. However, one wretched portaloo for about 1200 fans, many of whom had partaken of liquid refreshment, is not really acceptable.

I speak from first hand experience, having felt the need to visit this temporary (I trust) edifice after about half an hour of the match. As I commenced to relieve myself I noticed that the neighbouring, and only other, receptacle appeared to be blocked and was in danger of tipping its steaming, tawny coloured contents on to the floor and maybe even on to me. As this thought pressed the panic button in my mind, the portaloo was buffeted by another gale force wallop and the choppy waters of the blocked receptacle burst their banks, so to speak. Fortunately, my evasive action meant that only limited damage was suffered. I was just about to conclude my business in that rather unpleasant environment when a youngish County fan, who had undoubtedly spent the earlier part of that afternoon on licensed premises, joined me in the portaloo.

"Crap match, innit?" he said affably, and proceeded to pee into the unsavoury liquid which was just below the rim of the bowl.

"I've certainly seen better," I replied, leaving my fellow fan to his own devices as quickly as I could. As I stepped outside, another massive gust of wind rocked the portaloo, provoking a screeched expletive from its lone occupant.

I braved the elements and returned to my place on the terraces to find that Preston were attacking, as they had been doing throughout the first half. This was in spite of the fact that they were playing against the storm force wind. It was at this moment that Damon Searle, as he went to boot the ball clear, got underneath it a bit more than he had intended. As a result the ball soared off almost into orbit. What goes up must come down. And so it did, somewhere about the edge of the Preston penalty area where Brett Angell headed the ball and several pieces of the Mir space station over the advancing goalkeeper and into the net.

The goal caused the tempo of the match to increase and, from that moment, it became quite an exciting encounter. A hard fought 2-1 victory earned County another trip to the lair of the Lawnmower Man and a lot of praise from their manager. Unfortunately, not long afterwards, they produced "the worst performance I've seen in all my years in the game".

This slagging off of the team (he used to moan like mad if the fans did it), together with the annoying tendency to grab hold of the announcer's microphone and go and psych up the fans in the Cheadle End, did not endear "Mystic" Megson to me. Neither did his reference to a fan who had dared to offer some criticism as a "lobotomy case".

I have to admit that he did well in his first season in charge and that some, by no means all, of his signings seem to be money well-spent. However, the style of football played in the 1996-97 season largely disappeared with the departure of Chris Marsden and the 1998-99 season hardly produced a decent match. It was also fairly obvious that all was not well behind the scenes. If your technique of staff management is inspired by Captain Bligh, then the outcome will be "Mutiny on the County".

22

Where Do We Go From Here?

The most optimistic answer to that question is probably "not very far for the time being at least". "Mystic" received quite a lot of criticism when he compared County to a Skoda trying to compete with more upmarket vehicles. This remark revealed a lack of knowledge about rally driving but it was easy to see what he was getting at. Perhaps the club had gone a division too far.

The biggest mistake would be to push the boat out too far and spend ridiculous sums of money in an attempt to break into the Premier League where we would undoubtedly struggle. The folly of that philosophy was never more obvious than in November 1999, when a Second Round Cup match between Preston North End and non-league Enfield attracted nearly twice the number of spectators as County's Division 1 fixture against Sheffield United.

If the club can continue to consolidate their position over the next few years, then progress can eventually be made. The signs are that Brendan Ellwood and his fellow directors are well aware of the fact that the most effective reforms in the long term are those that are introduced slowly. All Nationwide clubs would do well to ensure that they are not too vulnerable from a financial viewpoint as the message is coming through loud and clear from certain of the Premier League's wealthier clubs that we are not all that far away from witnessing the implementation of a European League. Where that would leave all the other clubs is a matter for conjecture at the moment. However, I am convinced that, before the next decade has passed, there will have been a major restructuring of the English league caused by the departure of several of the bigger Premier League clubs. The fans of those clubs, the ordinary fans that is, will probably watch their team mainly on satellite TV.

The future of the professional game in this country will lie mainly in the hands of clubs like County and those other clubs who have been our rivals for many years. The fans of teams like Rochdale, Scunthorpe, Darlington and all the smaller clubs which have spent most of their existence in the bottom two divisions of the Football League will probably be the only ones who attend "live" matches. By "attend" I mean that they will go under their own steam to support their favourite team and pay at the turnstile for the dubious privilege of watching them play in all types of weather. They will not go as guests of the particular financial institution or telecommunications company that is sponsoring the match to watch the game from the warmth of a hospitality lounge having partaken of a four-course meal beforehand. They will probably come away feeling desperate after a 4-0 home defeat administered by mediocre opposition but will return a fortnight later full of an insane optimism. Long may they continue to do so and long may their teams be there for them.

Also of interest:

STOCKPORT COUNTY: An A to Z

Dean Hayes

If you follow Stockport County, then this is for you! From Abandoned Matches to Zenith, this book is packed with photographs, stories, and facts arranged alphabetically for easy reference. Almost 300 entries - including biographies of important players and managers - ensure that almost any question about the Hatters can be authoritatively answered.

£6.95

BLEAK & BLUE: 22 years at the Manchester Academy of Football Farce

Craig Winstanley

A great read for all Blues fans and for football fans everywhere, Bleak and Blue is a hugely entertaining record of the joys and misery of two decades of the history of Manchester City Football Club. A big book in every way, the author's fanzine-style writing covers all major games in minute detail, relentlessly pursuing a club which could again be a great football club. "An essential book for all Blues fans; and for all football fans....It's a brilliant read, even if you know nothing about football." SOUTH MANCHESTER REPORTER. £8.95

All of our books are available through booksellers. In case of difficulty, or for a free catalogue, please contact:

SIGMA LEISURE, 1 SOUTH OAK LANE, WILMSLOW, CHESHIRE SK9 6AR.

Phone: 01625-531035
Fax: 01625-536800.
E-mail: info@sigmapress.co.uk
Web site: http//www.sigmapress.co.uk

MASTERCARD and VISA orders welcome.